B2B Sales Mentors

20 STORIES FROM 20 TOP 1% SALES PROFESSIONALS

SCOTT INGRAM

Published by: Top 1% Publishing, Austin, Texas top1.fm/publishing

Disclaimer: The material in this publication is of the nature of general comment only, and does not represent professional advice. It is not intended to provide specific guidance for particular circumstances and it should not be relied on as the basis for any decision to take action or not take action on any matter which it covers. Readers should obtain professional advice where appropriate, before making any such decision. To the maximum extent permitted by law, the author and publisher disclaim all responsibility and liability to any person, arising directly or indirectly from any person taking or not taking action based on the information in this publication.

Cover design by: Tomsha Design

Book design by: Alex Head

ISBN: 978-0-9906059-7-3

This book is dedicated to those who generously supported the crowdfunding campaign that made the first Sales Success Stories book possible. It's thanks to their support and the success of that book that made this book possible. And to Dr. G.A. (Jahan) Mozaffarian, who we lost during the writing of this book. He gave the world an incredible and inspiring daughter.

Thank you:

Chris McNeill, Jerald Welch, Nader Shwayhat, Caitlyn Boger, M.K., Troy Odenwald, Andy Jaffke, Eduardo "Eddie" Baez, Sandra Thomas, Jeff Bajorek, Vlad Polikhun, Renee Tarrant, Kyle Porter, Todd Venable, David Scher, Lynda Dahlheimer, Aaron Johnson, Christie Walters, Greg Drose, Jim Riviello, Ron Masi, Karl Rego, Kevin Hall, Johnathan "Johnnie" Rudloff, Rachid Zidani, Colin Specter, Scott Lawrence, Dave Schwartz, Mary Jo McCarthy, Andrej Spisiak, Ernie Baer, Leila Mozaffarian, James Christman, Vito Fabiano and Ed Roberts

If you'd like to support the next volume of Sales Success Stories, get early access, and have your name listed in the next book, then be sure to join the reader list at top1.fm/B2Bbook

TABLE OF CONTENTS

INTRODUCTION

While this book is over one hundred pages long, it's basically a sampler. The first ten stories have been taken from the more extensive Volume 1 of the Sales Success Stories book, which features 60 Stories from 20 Top 1% Sales Professionals. The second set of stories are a preview of the upcoming second volume of this series, and is scheduled to be released October 15, 2019.

I really have two goals for this book. First, I hope it delivers a very high value to price ratio. We're charging way less than we probably should for this book which has some pretty unique content, to make these stories accessible. Each story comes from a real, top performing B2B sales professional. The top 1% designation isn't just a marketing ploy either. Every seller that you're about to hear from has recently been either the outright #1 performer on their team, or they have been in the top 1% in terms of quota attainment on a very large sales team.

The second goal is to introduce you to the other content and experiences that we have created specifically for B2B sales professionals, and the vast majority of that content is available to you for free. Starting with the Sales Success Stories Podcast (top1.fm) where you'll find deep dive interviews with every individual who has contributed to this compilation and new interviews that exclusively feature top 1%, quota-carrying individual contributors, being released every two weeks.

Also, you can meet, network with and learn from many of the individuals who have been on the podcast at our annual Sales Success Summit (Top1Summit.com) the second edition of that event will be in Austin, Texas October 14-15, 2019. This event is very intimate, and there are less than 200 tickets available. It was also built specifically for individual contributors who are committed to investing in themselves, their growth and have a desire to improve their results significantly. When you join the mailing list at top1.fm, I will happily send you the video of your choice from the 2018 Sales Success Summit.

Finally, there's the brand new Daily Sales Tips Podcast and Blog (DailySales.Tips) where you'll find an actionable idea from a variety of sales practitioners, sales leaders, authors, and others thought leaders in just 5-10 minutes or less, seven days a week.

Nobody will benefit more from your growth as a sales performer than you. May you discover the insights, ideas, and inspiration from these B2B Sales Mentors that you need to help get you to the next level.

THE MINDSET OF A CHAMPION

By Kyle Gutzler

Kyle Gutzler currently lives in San Francisco and works as an Enterprise Account Executive at Teradata. He previously worked in sales roles at Ecolab and Payscale. You can hear his full interview in episode 14 of the *Sales Success Stories* Podcast (top1.fm/14) and read his two other stories: Momentum Selling and Career Momentum in Volume 1 of the Sales Success Stories book.

After writing the viral blog post about how I doubled my sales on LinkedIn (top1.fm/2x), I also wrote another successful post which talked about a topic that is arguably more important to me than anything in sales - my mindset.

There are plenty of tips, tactics, and skills out there that will incrementally help with your sales success, but what you need to have more than anything to be a stellar sales professional is a rock-solid mindset. I came up with four keys which I'd like to unpack a bit further.

1. Why Not Me?

This is a question that I gathered from my hometown sports star, quarterback Russell Wilson. Whether or not you are a fan of Russell Wilson, you have to respect his story. He was passed up by many teams in the NFL draft as an undersized athlete that most teams didn't have faith in. He was finally selected as the 75th overall pick for the Seattle Seahawks, initially slated as a backup quarterback. He battled his way into the pre-season and eventually earned the starting spot. In just his second season in the NFL, he turned around a struggling franchise and brought his team all the way to the Super Bowl. His motto throughout the year was "why not me?" or "why not us?"

The Seahawks won that Super Bowl in a dominant fashion. I just couldn't get over this unusual, optimistic mindset that he led with. This is a mindset that I've always tried to mirror as a sales professional. I don't consider myself someone who has any superior gifts or natural talents. My advantage in sales is often in the reckless belief and faith that I can achieve greatness. In fact, at the company that I currently work for, one of my colleagues once said to me, "You probably think that you can do anything, don't you?" My answer was, and always will be, "yes." I've come to learn in my career that you will become what you believe. In the midst of a struggling season in sales, if you believe that you are incapable and that you cannot be a top sales professional, then that's what you will get. However, if you relentlessly fixate your mind on being a winner and being an elite performer, in time, that's what you will eventually become. Start thinking positive thoughts, write them down, verbalize them to others, and soon those things will begin to manifest themselves. Why not you?

2. Removing Marble

I shared a story in my post about the famous sculpture of David which was created by Michelangelo. It was said that Michelangelo described this process as simply taking away pieces of the stone that didn't resemble David. People are often curious about what you should do in sales to get better, what you should add to your process, or what prospecting tip you should try next time. However, it's equally important to address the things that you shouldn't do and what you should remove too. It's important to audit who you spend your time with as well. Are these people high performers? Are they positive and optimistic people? I've been in plenty of situations at work where I find myself hanging out with low-performers who radiate constant negativity. These people are absolutely toxic to you and you need to remove them from the rhythm of your day. It's also vital that you reflect on your own sales process. At my previous company, I spent a lot of time listening to recordings of myself. It's amazing how many quirks you will find that need adjustment. The headline here is that success in sales isn't just about addition; it's about subtraction too. Subtract the things that are holding you back from being great.

3. Patience and Persistence

I put the two of these together because you can't do one without the other and be successful. I was watching a video recently of a successful businessman named David Meltzer. To summarize his video, he was talking about how people need to look at "no" differently. He talked about how differently we would behave if we knew that behind our next 20 "nos" there was our next billion-dollar business idea. This was, of course, a radical example, but one of the big takeaways here is that people often give up too quickly. At my previous company, had I given up when the going got tough, it would have been a sad chapter for me in my career. Instead, I pushed past all the discomfort and rejection and eventually had my breakthrough which catapulted my career. However, to emphasize my original point, it's not just a game of waiting. You have to persist! Most of you know many of the fundamental keys to be successful in sales, now it's simply a matter of hammering away, over and over, until you finally break through and begin fulfilling your true potential.

4. Fire

If you've ever watched a survival show or been in a survival situation yourself, you know that fire is one of the top priorities. Fire is what makes all basic survival necessities possible. It allows you to purify water, cook food and stay warm. I think of fire as a symbol of success in my sales career. You can have all the knowledge, connections and skills imaginable, but if you don't have fire, you'll have a hard time being successful. To me, fire symbolizes a combination of passion, enthusiasm, and inspiration. What's interesting about fire is that you can have a strong flame that will eventually go out if it's not fueled with more wood. You've probably experienced this in your own life where sometimes you feel inspired and on top of the world, but as time passes, your flame begins to weaken. There are two primary things that I consistently do to spark a strong fire and also maintain the flame. First, I constantly remind myself of where I'm going by writing down my goals. If you're constantly living off the conditions of here and now, then your emotions will most certainly be a rollercoaster. Life will give you ups and downs, which is no secret. Therefore, it's human nature to react to what life is dealing you in the present moment. As a result, I try to fixate my mind on the exciting plans, goals, and dreams that I have for the future. This doesn't mean that I don't celebrate the wins that happen here and now, but if I lose out on a $500,000 deal, it's a lot easier to swallow if I've convinced myself that one day I'll close a $500,000,000 deal. Secondly, I prioritize relationships over everything. The attitude of those who you spend your time with is contagious. I know that if I manage the circle of people that I surround myself with and keep hanging out with A-players, then I'll have a much easier time sustaining my fire. In fact, I try to make it a habit of reaching out to others and encouraging my network when I myself am struggling. If I'm going through a rough season, my default reaction is to lift other people up. Helping those that I care about has always helped me, plain and simple.

Lessons Learned:

- Thoughts become things. You've probably heard this phrase before. I'm completely subscribed to this notion. I've learned that at the end of the day, I have the choice of how I think. It's been proven that what you fixate your mind on and what you believe tend to become a reality. Knowing this, I may as well be recklessly faith-filled in my abilities, my likelihood to win, and my chances of being successful.

- Don't just pile on new learnings, tactics, and methodologies. Take inventory of your behavior and figure out what things you need to cut out in order to help you be a more successful sales professional. This could be related to how you spend your time, what you say in sales meetings, or even who you surround yourself with.

- It's completely normal to face rejection and failure. Once you understand that this is part of the game, simply be persistent and stay patient and you will undoubtedly reach success.

- Consistently remind yourself of the big things that you are working toward.

- Never stop pouring into the important relationships in your life.

I'M 6'4" AND DEVILISHLY HANDSOME

By Trong Nguyen

With more than 20 years of experience Trong Nguyen honed his craft at Digital Equipment Corporate (HP), IBM, Dell and Microsoft. Currently, he works with Anaplan and has been on the podcast twice. First in episode 25 (top1.fm/25) and again in episode 46 (top1.fm/46). He's written two books of his own: *Winning the Cloud* and *Winning the Bank* in addition to the three other stories he contributed to Volume 1 of *Sales Success Stories*: The Playa, What Are You Scared Of? And Why Lunch Doesn't Matter

When you talk to sales managers or the VPs of Sales, they always ask the same questions: "Do you have relationships with the CXO? What's your relationship with the CXO? How can you close that deal without the CXO's support?"

These questions are not in the wrong; I just don't think they're very helpful. If they just pivot a little bit, the whole conversation changes. What I would ask is: "How can we develop relationships with the CXO?" When you start asking that question, it inevitably lends itself to deeper thought and introspection.

Most sales reps take a very binary approach to relationships – they are on or off. They either have these relationships or they don't, at least in their minds. Invariably this perspective leads them down a linear approach to addressing the issue at hand. If they don't have a relationship with the CXO, then they go out of their way to build that relationship directly. They invite the CXO to social events, dinners, and whatever else they can in the hopes that these bonding moments will lead to future sales.

Direct strategies are useful in certain situations, but not all of them. I would submit that there may be a better way to build these executive relationships. Instead of going at it head-on, I want to provide you with a framework in which to think about how you can develop and influence your relationships. This framework is applicable in your personal life as well as your business life. It's applicable whether you are a customer-facing sales representative or if your work function is internal facing.

In the 1960s, industrial psychologists David Merrill and Roger Reid did an extensive study around dimensions of assertiveness and responsiveness. From that study, they came up with a 2x2 matrix outlining four social styles: analytical, driving, expressive, and amiable. When I first read the study, I wept for days; I was overcome with joy. Forget SpaceX or Tesla, this revelation was akin to Elon Musk harnessing his brilliance in physics and engineering to find a way of creating hickory smoked bacon out of thin air.

Here's the practical application of this theory:

1. **Step 1:** Perform a personality analysis on the CXO, senior executive, or any person you want to build a relationship with, and then place them in one of the four quadrants.

2. **Step 2:** Then, look at all of the people that influence that person. Perform a personality analysis on those people and place them into the appropriate quadrants.

3. **Step 3:** Now think about all of the people that influence the people that influence the client. Do a personality analysis on those people and place them into the right quadrants.

4. **Step 4:** Complete a relationship alignment exercise. Find the right people in your organization to connect to all of those people you have identified and start building up those relationships.

Here is the execution of the process in its visual form.

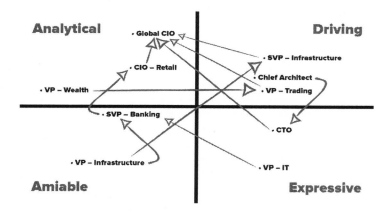

Over time, what you have essentially done is executed a complete surround strategy. The main reason why this strategy works is that you are not dependent on one person for success or failure. In our highly matrixed world, decisions are made by committees or groups of people. That's why this strategy has been so successful over time.

I was working with a global manufacturing company based in Chicago and I executed this strategy to build the right relationships with the Global CIO. Along the way, I had built relationships with the VP of Architecture, SVP of Operations, SVP of Infrastructure, etc. It took me six months and I hadn't spent any time with the Global CIO at all.

Instead of shooting for the moon right away, I first built a ladder to the clouds.

By now I had solved numerous complex issues for this company and had built up my brand as a creative problem solver and Mr. Fixit. It didn't matter if you had hardware issues, software issues, or more. With some duct tape, vinegar, and a pair of chopsticks, I could make MacGyver look bad. I completely influenced those who would influence the Global CIO.

With my reputation now in the bag, I asked the Chief Technology Officer to introduce me to the Global CIO. When I went to the meeting, she said something to me that I will never forget. She said, "Trong, after all of the great stories I had heard about you, I just pictured you would be 6'4" and devilishly handsome."

I told her I was! It was the start of an enduring and beneficial relationship.

Lessons Learned:

- Developing senior executive relationships takes time. Focus on strategies that develop these long-term relationships. Like all relationships, trust is earned, and it is earned over time.

- If an executive tells you how powerful they are in the company, they aren't. The only ones that tell you that are the insecure ones who aren't the real decision makers. Einstein didn't have to go around telling people how smart he was - you just knew.

- Be genuine and authentic. Smart people will see right through people who aren't genuine. If you don't like sports, don't pretend to be a sports fan just to impress a customer. Find some other common ground to build the relationship on.

- Influence those who would influence the relationships you want to develop.

- Perform a personality analysis to understand the person you want to develop a relationship with so that you understand their motivations and what makes them "tick."

- Use multiple approaches for building relationships. These include direct, indirect, and surround strategies.

- Focus on adding value, as that will be the foundation for long-term relationships.

- Network and build relationships well before you need them. When the time comes, they will be more open to helping you.

- Integrity is non-negotiable; work only with people of integrity. Steer clear of those people who are morally ambiguous.

- Leadership styles and approaches change over time. A leader who was good for a particular time and situation may not be suited to other circumstances.

BEST PRACTICES VS. ONLY PRACTICES

By Paul DiVincenzo

Paul DiVincenzo just joined Gartner after spending the last 12 years with Cintas in Southern California. He was featured in Episode 40 of the podcast (top1.fm/40) and contributed three other stories to Volume 1 of *Sales Success Stories*: People to People Sales, Success from Relationships and Trust, and Getting Promoted in Tough Times

Many of these terms should sound familiar to you if you've been in sales or business for any length of time…. Let's see if you recognize some of them: best practices, role plays, phone block, activity, leaderboards, KPIs. I have been lucky enough to be a top seller in two Fortune 500 companies over the past 15 years of my sales career. Every day, I have someone ask me what my Best Practices are for prospecting, selling, managing my numbers, career matters, etc... I usually let them know it's not that easy and that they should focus on the fundamentals for now. Recently, I've been thinking about what I do that really does make a difference. Obviously, my sales success has come with a lot of hard work and with that, some great recognition internally at the companies I've worked for. It's interesting to watch the same lingo go around and around, mostly by sales leadership and, in many cases, businesspeople in general.

The one that stands out to me which offers a significant improvement for people that are looking to excel in sales is best practices... The reality of sales is that if you stick to the standards of activity, follow up, professionalism, and great manners, you should be *pretty successful*. However, if you really want to go from average to being consistently at the top, it takes creating something called "only" practices. This means creating significant differences between what ONLY YOU can or will do for the customer and the sale. It will push you ahead of your internal and external competition for sustained success. I can't remember where I heard this term originally, but when I did, I knew right away that's exactly how I've been in the top 10% year over year for almost 17 years. I didn't know what I did differently from any other salespeople for many years. However, after thinking about it, the short answer is that I am willing to do more for my customers than anybody else every time to exceed my numbers and make as much money as possible for me and my family.

When I first started in sales at the Cintas uniform sales division, I took over a territory in the Palm Springs California market which was heavily driven toward hospitality. This includes many hotels and resorts. I focused primarily on selling customers uniforms as a service; this means that the company rents uniforms for their employees vs. purchasing them. We pick up and deliver uniforms each week, as well as wash, clean, inspect, and repair or replace them to a condition that is wearable and acceptable in a hotel environment. Many of these hotels are 4-5 star resorts. This service has a lot of attention to detail and the back end of the business is highly standardized. In other words, we have a very small and limited selection of uniforms, compared to the purchase options, and when it comes down to design elements such as color patterns, there weren't a lot of options. It's a bit of a joke in the industry, however, it's really true, as you can only carry so many colors and maintain that inventory at a profit level that makes sense. I was selling to the Hyatt Grand Champion resort in the Indian Wells area of Palm Springs California. Although they had some maintenance people that would wear our standard uniforms, I was told by the Director of Rooms that the housekeeping department (typically a purchase-only program) wanted to chat with me, as they wanted to wear dresses with matching aprons along with a Hawaiian pattern that needed to be sewn into the garment to match some of the decor in the hotel. By the way, they didn't want to purchase it; they wanted to rent it and have me offer it as a uniform as a service…! As I heard the customer describe what they wanted, I almost fell out of my chair, because this was unheard of in our industry. There were so many hurdles that I simply didn't know where to start; however, the total opportunity in the sale could cover my sales number for just under a full year of sales. Because I was in such shock, it was actually a positive in the strategy. I didn't talk at all during the meeting; I simply listened, took notes and let the general manager of the Hyatt know that I would find a way to make this happen. His eyes lit up when I said that, because later I found out he had met with every other uniform company in our area, including a rep from Cintas, that all said no just as quickly as I said I would find a way to make it happen. We shook hands and I left the office, almost passing out in the 115° heat in the Coachella Valley area of Palm Springs. This project was so far outside the norm that I didn't know how I would get it done. It included learning about sourcing garments from across the country and outside the country, working with designers to have a pattern made, and gaining consensus internally that our company would produce this garment with a sufficient enough quantity for us to rent it (I didn't know any of this at the time).

I called my sales manager and let him know we had an opportunity to close one deal that could cover almost my full year of sales quota/projections and that it was going to take something extraordinary for us to get it. He didn't have a clue what was about to happen. I went home that evening to my newborn son, who was only about 2 ½ years old at the time, and I thought to myself, *you have to make this happen, you will make this happen, you will find a way.*

In the following weeks after the meeting, I began to educate myself on all the capabilities of Cintas beyond my day-to-day selling job. I investigated what our supply chain opportunities were, where the dress was being manufactured, how long it took for the dress to be manufactured, and how much fabric it would take to create the trim and all the other elements. However, I had no clue what they were prior to that meeting. I had conference calls with designers, conference calls with manufacturing, conference calls with distribution and maintained engagement with those people, letting them guide me with their expertise. As I went through this process, I gained significant experience beyond what I would normally garner and have been able to use that knowledge for over a decade after that for sale in many other sales. This knowledge has allowed me to stand out from anybody inside my company or from competition about this particular category of our business. I didn't know at the time, but this is a key component to my overall success in not hesitating to jump in and learn a significant amount of information beyond my normal job scope, which will create a unique expertise for me that I can offer as value to my potential customers and current customers. Pushing yourself into the unknown is the best way to create "only" practices for yourself that you can then have for future use against your competition.

After my month-long education in the garment business, I was able to gather up all the information necessary to put together a business model, present that internally at Cintas, and create a pricing structure that didn't exist prior to the sale. I then went to the customer and was able to explain to them all the elements going into their production model, including hard goods design elements, and tie that back into how they wanted their resort to stand out from the vision created by the general manager. They didn't hesitate when I proposed a custom pricing structure that ended up being *four times higher* than any other program in the marketplace. I had delivered as promised. They approved it within two weeks including a multiyear agreement for services. I made Presidents Club my first year with Cintas that year, as well as rookie of the quarter and rookie of the year. That singular experience created a foundation of "doing whatever it takes" that I have utilized consistently in hundreds of other sales over the course of my 15+ year career with the company. This has helped me earn Presidents Club and Diamond Level recognition for multiple years and has allowed me to be fearless when it comes to looking into the future, creating something new and highly valuable for the company and my customers. Every day I'm creating, looking, and executing on only practices. By using this strategy consistently, I have been able to uncover new markets for the company, create new positions for myself within the company, and gain promotions and salary increases over the course of my career that other people have not been able to accomplish. This has not only allowed me to be in the top-selling rankings in my company; this has also allowed me to be viewed by the executives as a leading contributor to the growth of the organization.

Lessons Learned:

- Never lower your or the customers' expectations.

- Say Yes and figure it out for the customer.

- This will push you to learn more.

- By learning more and being resourceful you'll gain experience, tools, and resources which you can re-use to leapfrog your competition (other reps and competitors).

- Create and track your "only" practices from these experiences and push to expand those so that you will be offering experiences, knowledge, expertise, and the ability to execute on it where your competition will still be speaking features, benefits, and lower pricing.

SET YOUR GOALS AT 2X TO 3X YOUR QUOTA AND BUILD A DAILY ROUTINE TO OVER ACHIEVE

By Trey Simonton

Trey Simonton was recently promoted to Vice President of Regional Sales at Accruent. Throughout his career, he has worked in a variety of roles from business development to global accounts at enterprise technology companies. Trey was featured in Episode 35 (top1.fm/35) of the podcast and contributed the stories: Make a Habit of Biting Your Tongue, So the Client has Time to Speak and Take Time to Research and Always do a Dry Run to Volume 1 of *Sales Success Stories*.

We all hear about the importance of setting our goals high, but I struggled for many years to understand what that meant, and how to create a plan to overachieve on my quota. As a seasoned sales rep, I've watched many of the best focus on their numbers. They dissect their territory well and seem always to have a plan to quickly exceed their quota, get into accelerators and make some real money. That's why we do what we do – right?!

A better way of managing this process became very clear in January of 2010. I had just attended a conference where Mark Allen, six-time Ironman Triathlon World Champion, spoke about his struggle to be one of the best tri-athletes of all time. Mark shared that although for years he dominated in triathlons around the globe, he continuously finished behind Dave Scott at the Ironman Triathlon World Championship in Kona, Hawaii. Mark shared that to be a World champion and to beat Dave Scott; he had to change his diet, training and focus to be the best. Mark's talk got me thinking that maybe I needed to step back and change my approach to sales.

When I returned to the office that year, we were in the middle of territory planning. Instead of doing what I always did, I took a different approach and scheduled a meeting with my sales operations team. I asked for detailed stats on my average deal size the prior year and the average deal size of the broader sales team. I requested conversion rates for how many emails it took on average across the team to get to one sales call, and how many calls it took with a prospect before it created an opportunity. With that information, my close rates were easy to understand; this helped me set weekly goals around the pipeline I needed to achieve my higher goals. I wanted to look at my sales activity as a math problem.

My Quota	$1,200,000
My Personal Goal	$2,400,000
Pipeline Required (4x based on close rates)	$9,600,000
Pipeline Required per Week (50 Weeks)	$ 192,000
Deals Needed to Hit Goal (Average Deal Size: $120,000)	approx. 20

Deals Needed in Pipeline (Close Rate: 27%)	approx. 80
Meetings needed to get to an Opp (Success Rate: 1 in 4)	4
Calls needed to schedule a meeting (Success Rate: 1 in 8)	8
Emails needed to secure a meeting (Success Rate: 1 in 32)	32

I took the time to back into what activities it would take daily to reach my higher annual sales goals. We all know that 4x pipeline is a good target for sales bookings. That number divided by 50 selling weeks helped me realized how much pipeline I needed to generate each week. Taking it a step further, my success rate for calls or meetings that turn into an opportunity was also one in four. As I dug deeper, I discovered that it took about 32 emails or about eight phone calls to generate one meeting.

Once I knew my numbers, I threw out any thought about my quota and created new habits and routines based on my personal annual sales goal. I have a wife and two children, so three days of the week, I got up an hour earlier and sent thirty-two emails and made eight phone calls. Most of the phone calls were messages, but I found prospects to be impressed that I was up earlier than they were.

The emails and phone calls became an obsession, but I believed in the numbers. I knew if I stuck with the routine. Eventually the pipeline would come. Early morning emails and calls required me to prepare the list of whom I wanted to contact and the messaging the night before. I even scheduled 90 minutes of time to myself every Sunday to get direction on whom I wanted to target and the message I wanted to share.

Over time, the pipeline started to come. I found that the way I spent my days was changing. I would have all my prospecting done by 6am before my daughter woke up and when I arrived at the office, my time was spent fielding client calls, preparing proposals and progressing deals. My productivity went through the roof!

As the end of the year approached, I was tracking towards $2.5 Million in sales. As often happens, a $300,000 deal pushed out into the following year, and I finished at $2.2 Million in sales – 92% of my $2.4 Million goal. Internally, I was devastated. I had changed my routines but failed to hit my sales goals.

Externally, I celebrated. I finished #3 out of 60 reps globally and made more money that year than I had made the two years prior. Further, I closed the last $300,000 deal in late January of the next year starting off my next selling year with real momentum.

I continue this routine today, knowing I must understand my numbers and set my goals high to be one of the best, for both myself and the company I represent.

CREATIVE PROSPECTING

By Scott Ingram

Scott Ingram is the host of the *Sales Success Stories* Podcast, the *Daily Sales Tips* Podcast and the top Account Director at Relationship One. He shared his own story in Episode 62 of the *Sales Success Stories* Podcast (top1.fm/62). He contributed three other stories in Volume 1 of *Sales Success Stories*: A Rapid Rise, and Epic Fall and Getting "Fired Up," Be Specific About What You Want and Getting it Done and Doing it Right - Recipe for a Great Sales Culture.

I learned a lot from my time at Bazaarvoice. They had one of the best sales cultures, as well as company cultures, that I've ever been a part of. Though to be fair, Eloqua was way up there as well, and it's probably no coincidence that both of those companies had successful Initial Public Offerings (IPOs).

At Bazaarvoice, where we brought ratings and reviews technology to many of the most successful online retailers and brands, the way we engaged prospective clients through the entire sales cycle was really something special. We demanded maximum creativity and personalization from hyper-relevant outreach lead by our team of Market Developers (what the rest of the world now calls Sales Development Reps or SDRs) all the way through to new client celebrations. Importantly, these were as much about the client as they were about the sales win. We would often have clients on the line to celebrate with us as we hit a 42" gong and told the story of our newest client and how we were going to make them even more successful together.

This creative client-story-focused way of connecting was contagious and is something I've worked hard to bring to my own sales efforts ever since. Let me tell you about one of my favorite prospecting stories, as it was a ton of fun and I can also share the resulting photo with you at the end.

One of the companies in my northeastern US-focused territory was Steve Madden, the shoe company. My market developer, Alvie, and I had been trying to get through to their head of e-commerce with no success. Now, I can't recall exactly how we learned about this opportunity, but somehow, we found out that Steve Madden was going to be making a personal appearance at a Nordstrom's here in Austin. I knew we couldn't pass up the opportunity, so Alvie and I put our heads together and came up with a solid plan.

Fast forward a few weeks, as Alvie and I waited in line together on a Saturday morning for an hour or so for our chance to meet, and more importantly, get our picture taken with, Steve Madden. We had made a rather large sign that simply had 5 stars on it to represent the favorable customer ratings and the impact they would bring to the company's online sales efforts.

When we got to the front of the line, we asked Steve to hold the sign while we got our picture taken with him. He was a little apprehensive about what we were going to do with the picture, but we briefly explained what we did and what we were trying to do. This certainly wasn't the time for a detailed pitch, so he agreed to the photo and we were on our way.

We had a lot of fun using that photo in our subsequent interactions with the organization. I believe the initial response that came just a few minutes after we sent the photo to our targeted marketing executive was something along the lines of: "Well, one way or another, you managed to get a picture with my boss. I'm pretty sure I have to take the meeting now."

The image then worked its way into every subsequent presentation and they always enjoyed hearing the story of what we did to get it.

Lessons Learned:

- It's rarely easy to break through and get the attention of a cold prospect. Taking a creative, unique, and personalized approach improves your odds exponentially.

- Featuring a company's own brand (or executives) in your outreach can set you apart.

- Sales can be a grind. Be creative and have some fun. At the very least, it'll make for a great story later.

DIFFERENTIATING YOURSELF FROM THE AVERAGE SALES DEVELOPMENT REP (SDR)

By Florin Tatulea

Florin Tatulea was the top Sales Development Rep at Loopio in Toronto when he spoke with Scott in Episode 22 (top1.fm/22) and has since been promoted to Account Executive. Florin was once a nationally ranked Tennis Player in Canada and contributed two other stories to Volume 1 of *Sales Success Stories*: The Art of Persistence and Knowing When to Quit and Always be A/B Testing.

B ecoming one of the best in any particular discipline is not easy, but starts with having belief in yourself first and foremost. It sounds cliché, but this is much easier said than done. I'm talking about the belief where every ounce of you to the core believes in what you are setting out to do and no external doubt or person can influence you otherwise.

If you ask any single person if they think they are better than average, most will tell you that they are. The truth though, is that most people have a fear of success and only artificially believe in themselves.

The moment that a negative person or external circumstance challenges that belief, the self-doubt begins to set in because they weren't fully bought into themselves and their purpose to the core.

The fear of success is something I've personally struggled with; this stems from self-doubt in thinking that one is not special nor worthy of remarkable things.

The funny thing is that the average person, or SDR in this case, is really not that good at all. The things that consistently distinguish an average SDR from a top SDR are very minor things.

This is true in any aspect of life. Take tennis, for example, the things that separate Roger Federer from the 100th best player in the world are minor details. If you were to see Federer rallying with the 100th best player in a warm up, it would be nearly impossible to distinguish who was better.

However, the extra practice, the extra footwork sessions, and the extra morning visualization sessions add up over time to allow Federer to execute on the one point in the match that matters most.

There is so much noise in the sales development world today and prospects are becoming increasingly difficult to reach. TOPO reports that it now takes an average of 18 dials to connect with a buyer (Source: top1.fm/TOPOsdtech) and The Bridge Group reports that the number of attempts per prospect has risen consistently from 4.7 in 2010 to 9.1 in 2018, while the number of quality conversations per day has decreased from 8.0 to 5.1 during the same period of time. (Source: top1.fm/BGsdrmetrics)

This means that to break away from the crowd, you now have to be (a little) more creative.

Here are 7 (small) things you can do to differentiate yourself as an SDR in 2018.

1. Use Video in your Outreach

Although incorporating video in cadences is gaining traction and becoming more common, it still hasn't hit the mainstream. There is still time to use this method as a means of personalizing your outreach and standing out.

GoVideo by Vidyard is a free Chrome extension which allows you to record, send, and track customized videos to your prospects.

I have used GoVideo on a daily basis and have booked many meetings that may have never happened because I went above and beyond what most prospects had ever seen.

The content in your videos does not have to be anything revolutionary (if you want to be in the top 10%). Don't use a script; be your genuine self. Discuss a couple of points, showing that you have done your research, and use a verbal call to action at the end.

As an extra tip, I recommend keeping videos below 60 seconds in length and having a name card with your prospect's name as the thumbnail, so that they can tell it's customized.

If you want to get into the top 1%, you should go above and beyond. For example, you can create fully customized videos recording yourself singing a song for your prospect or tying in an analogy about their favorite sports team into your pitch and call-to-action.

2. Send physical cards or packages

Calls, e-mails, and social channels are becoming increasingly saturated. A good way to stand out in 2018 is by going the traditional route and sending hand-written cards, gifts, or sentimental packages.

Examples of packages we have sent include:
-Hand-written cards
-Edible Arrangements
-Cupcakes
-Toy Cars (prospect joked about wanting a luxury car, we sent it!)
-Company Swag

There are solutions in the market, like a company called PFL (top1. fm/pfl) which automates the process of mailing customized physical gifts through your CRM system.

Another creative thing to send is Piñatas through www.pina-tagrams.com.

3. Cold Call outside of business hours

Analyze when the best time to call your ideal target prospects is and block that time out in your calendar. Typically, the best hours for cold calling are before the work day begins and as things are winding down towards the end of the day.

Being the best takes sacrifice, so figure out a schedule that works for you and wake up early if you have to. Stay late and bang out those calls. If you want to be average and are just looking for a way to fund your social life, feel free to work a 9-5, that's cool too!

4. Use Owler/LinkedIn/Alerts/Company websites to tailor your email outreach

If your prospects' replies are along the lines of "Unsubscribe," you are not customizing your emails enough. I have tried so many different approaches throughout my time as an SDR and the best results I have gotten have always been when I customized each touch point.

Ever since I eliminated template-style emails, I have received 0 "unsubscribe" replies and plenty of replies praising me for the amount of research/customization that I have done. The truth is that I don't do any kind of "revolutionary" research…it really only takes 5-10 minutes to craft an email that shows that you actually care, which causes you to stand out.

LinkedIn
Once you know which account you are prospecting, go on LinkedIn, find your ideal prospects, see if they liked/shared any interesting posts or what groups/interests they include in their profile. Also, go to the company's page and see what kind of growth they have experienced in the last

couple of years. This could be a good indicator that they are in growth mode and most likely in need of solutions to help automate processes. Use this information and craft a 1-2 sentence introduction.

Owler

Owler is a tool that scrapes the web and finds all relevant news articles/ press releases on the account. At Loopio, we use Salesloft as our email automation platform and Owler is built directly into the platform. Owler allows you to learn about recent rounds of funding and press releases that talk about interesting product updates/events/awards happening within the relevant company. You can also use this information to craft a 1-2 sentence introduction too.

Company Website

You know best what indicators determine whether an account is a good fit. For us, the industries our prospects sell into are a good indicator. Therefore, I go on their website and look through their customers' page and find out what industries they sell into. You can also use this information to write a more customized introduction sentence.

Google Alerts

You can set up Google Alerts to get notified as soon as news comes out about certain prospects, companies, competitors etc. Use these alerts as potential trigger events to reach out to your prospects.

5. Send outreach emails on evenings and weekends

Similar to calling during off-peak hours, you also have a higher chance of getting opens on emails when the volume of emails hitting a prospect's inbox is low.

Most SDRs are not going to be sending emails after 6 pm during weekdays and on weekends. Take advantage of this fact and use your email automation platform to send your emails during these off-peak hours.

Try scheduling your emails **for 9 pm on weekdays or for 9 pm on a Sunday** when people are preparing for the week ahead.

6. Customize Connection requests on LinkedIn and don't include an ask right away

This, once again, comes down to sticking out from the crowd. Most SDRs are sending InMails and connection requests that immediately pitch the product/solution they are selling and have an ask from the prospect right away.

Instead of doing this, you should do a bit of research on the prospect. See if there are any personal/company milestones that you can congratulate them on without doing any initial selling.

Another approach is to have an insight about the industry the prospect is in and ask a question where the answer could set you up for a pitch.

For example:

> Hi [NAME],
> I noticed that your team/company is [STATE KEY POINT SHOWING YOU DID RESEARCH]. From my experience, that usually means that [PROVIDE INDUSTRY INSIGHT].
> Is that the case for your team?

7. The purpose of a voicemail is to direct your prospect to your email

Let's face it, voicemail reply rates are *extremely low*. The purpose of a voicemail should be to get your prospect to open your email where you have your value proposition. You only have a few seconds of your prospects' attention at this point and there is no time for a pitch.

Here is a nice template I have been using recently, which was recommended by Tito Bohrt and works well:

> Hi {{First Name}}, this is {{YOU!}} with {{company}}. I sent you an email yesterday about {{subject of email or topic covered}} but I have not heard back from you. Can you give it a quick glance and reply back? Again it's {{YOU!}} with {{company}}. Thanks!

This voicemail works because it teases some information and sparks the curiosity, which leads to the prospect going to your value-added email. It's important to restate your name at the end so that they can find the email in their inbox.

Lessons Learned:

1. The difference between the average SDR and the top ones are minor. However, minor tweaks over a long period of time lead to exponential results.

2. Always be looking to innovate; these 7 steps that work now may not work in two years. The important part is to acknowledge this and constantly push the boundaries of creative outreach.

3. In a world that is constantly changing and with technologies like AI coming into play, personalization and a focus on quality outreach will allow you to stand out and prevail.

DISCOVERY IS NOT JUST ONE STEP IN THE PROCESS

By Debe Rapson

Debe Rapson lives in the Bay Area and has over 30 years of sales experience. Currently, she works with Sprinklr in an Enterprise Account role and was featured in Episode 11 of the podcast (top1.fm/11). Also, she wrote the story: Courage Drives Positive Outcomes in Volume 1 of *Sales Success Stories*.

During my thirty years in sales, I have honed the science and art of my discovery process to ensure that when I ask for the business, it never falls flat. Today, decisions are made through consensus and unlike the past, discovery is not done solely with one or two key stakeholders, but rather everyone on the decision team, typically between 8 to 12 people.

Coming to those discussions with a thorough understanding of the company's firmographics, both corporate initiatives and strategies will familiarize you with a high-level overview of the company's current state. Luckily, we have many easy ways to conduct such research today, and the best salespeople do their legwork before they ever reach out to ask for the meeting. Educating oneself about a prospective company prior to meeting with it is absolutely crucial to the sales process and can boost one's odds of landing a sale by leaps and bounds, as opposed to meeting with a prospect cold. I always look at a company's annual report and 10-K and spend time researching presentations on the web delivered by the key stakeholders and executives that will be making the decision. This enables me to understand their goals, challenges, ideologies, pipeline projects, etc. Furthermore, in order to figure out "who's who in the zoo," I conduct research on discover.org and LinkedIn. When I familiarize myself with a company's technology stack, I reference sites similar to builtwith.com. Other sites such as Detective by Charlie, Demandbase, and LinkedIn help me to unearth relevant topical information quickly. Lastly, before I sit down with a prospect, I follow those stakeholders on Twitter and their company on Facebook so that I can learn what they comment and care about on social media.

Today, information is easily available, so there is no reason for a salesperson not to be able to ask the probing questions that will help both the seller and prospective client. Perhaps the most important piece of advice that I can offer is not to be lazy in the preliminary stages of the sale cycle.

The job of the salesperson has changed dramatically over the past twenty years, particularly the last five, where we've seen the pace of our sales cycles slow down, a huge increase of easily accessible information and more sales processes than ever before. Salespeople are trying to figure out how to close faster, take advantage of the knowledge available, and perfect their own process down to a science. However, what remains the same is that customers buy from "genuine" people. The quickest way to earn that trusted advisor relationship is by understanding "why" they are looking to make a change, "why" they are motivated to change and "why" the company is going to fund the change.

Early in my sales career, I created my own sales process which featured the most important step: discovery. I typically would develop an in-depth list of questions, taking a personal and conversational approach. My natural curiosity and passion would always propel us three levels deeper, and this is where you uncover the reason why they have to buy. At this time, I was selling services for a high-end, high-value computer training company. Back then, computer training was a competitive industry with many low-cost providers. We couldn't compete on price, but could always win on value because of our sheer size, talent, and innovative approach. A large travel services company in my territory was looking to procure computer training for all 10,000 employees and sent out a blind request for proposal.

As part of their process, we had a short window of opportunity to question the business stakeholder (let's call her Doris); this was my opportunity, but I knew I needed to stand out from the competition. I invited Doris to our office in San Francisco, so she could see us in action. I also asked one of our lead trainers to sit in on the discussion to help me ask all the right questions; he was the expert.

We asked Doris questions focusing on training delivery, her company's experience with a provider, their need for additional support, and why. We wanted to understand what the company was looking to accomplish with this investment and what failure and success would subsequently look like. We inquired how she got to be the project lead and what would make her look good to the executives. Her answers got us excited about this project and she could see that we were genuinely interested in helping them transform the skill set of their workforce. Our lead trainer suggested additional criteria that would make their project more successful and ensure that the computer training skills would stick. Our sixty-minute session grew into two hours as we asked deeper questions that morphed into a plan that would quickly add long-term value for their teams.

That discussion was the catalyst for a long-term relationship that began with creating a champion and establishing the framework for partnership with Doris.

We continued to align the things we learned that day with our differentiators. After we were awarded a multi-million dollar contract, Doris later told me that they felt heard that first day we met and we gave them confidence that we would deliver their desired outcome.

One can't solve problems without understanding "the why." At this point in my career, I hadn't yet developed my process, but it became clear to me that I stumbled upon a formula during this meeting that would forever change my approach to discovery.

Lessons Learned:

A well thought out discovery process does the following things for you:

- Determines whether an account is your ideal customer or is simply going to be a waste of your precious time and energy.

- Captures your customer's true needs and their definition of value to precisely match your solution to what they ideally would like to buy.

- Uncovers a prospect's complete decision-making process right from the start, allowing you to know exactly what you need to do each step of the way in order to win their business.

A well-thought-out discovery process does the following things for your prospect:

- Establishes a partnership approach.

- Helps them to uncover what they haven't thought about or didn't know.

- Establishes your credibility.

While conducting discovery....

- Be warm – develop rapport through common connections, interests & backgrounds.

- Be genuinely curious... People know when you are faking it.

- Establish credibility through storytelling – Know your facts.

- Gaint trust through listening and not selling.

- Be honest... If you can't solve their problem, tell then and make a suggestion.

Tips/Tricks for discovery:

- Enter every meeting prepared with everything you could find about the company.

- Take Great Notes/NOT on your computer-it's distracting and loud.

- Triangulate it with other key stakeholders.

- Deliver highly-personalized presentations with what you learned.

- Remind prospects of the value to them via objection handling.

- Hold them accountable to what they shared.

What if you could create so much value in your customer's mind that they would want your solution no matter what the price? This is how you do get it done....

THE YEAR I DOUBLED MY INCOME

By David Weiss

David Weiss is an Enterprise Sales Leader at ADP where he manages a team that sells strategic outsourcing to large enterprises. David was featured in Episode 24 of the podcast (top1.fm/24) and contributed two other stories to Volume 1 of the *Sales Success Stories* book: Don't Take it Personally; They Just Didn't Want to Buy From You and Just F@#$ing Kill Me. He's also about to release his own book: *Your Sales Career Guide* – A Must read for anyone new to sales, or thinking about a career in sales

Imagine for a second you are, at least in your mind, the best at something, and up to this point in your life, mostly, you have been proven correct. That was me, basking in my glorious ignorance. I had done some amazing things and had been living a sales career I was proud of. I had made consistent multiple six figure incomes, hit or exceeded plan every year at every company I had been part of, won multiple Presidents' Clubs to some of the best destinations in the world. I've hired and trained people who have hit their goals, and taken on initiatives that have helped to shape the strategy and culture of multiple organizations. I thought I was elite. I thought I had this sales thing figured out. Boy was I wrong.

At this point in my career, it was rare for me to get pushed, and pushed hard, on my sales ability. After all, I was successful, and working in a senior level sales role at a Fortune 250 company. I've read many books on sales, and as I mentioned in my other story, been trained by some great people and companies. After Aramark, I went on to Career-Builder, which has been consistently ranked as one of the best companies to sell for, with the best training, as has the Fortune 250 company I was working for at the time. However, along came a leader who flipped my world upside down. When Gregory Donovan was first assigned to my team, I took the approach of, "Who is this new guy and what can he do for me?" (As I get older, wiser and frankly realize how stupid I am, I have learned that it's important to allow people to challenge me, and this person did like no other). He had been a successful enterprise salesperson for years, started his own company and sold it, and was well connected with heads of sales at some huge companies. He quickly showed me I had much more room to grow.

Let me be humbly honest; there are times in sales or in anything, where you experience much success and you get complacent. You expect that your success will keep going, because why wouldn't it? You forget that to get where you have gotten, you had to earn it, DAILY. Not only did Gregory smack that reality back into me, but he also showed me how much more I could be doing, and in turn, how much more I could be making. He quickly, and in a rather stoic way, showed me he was the master and I was the student; he painted a new reality for me I had to achieve.

Ok, so how did he shake my foundation? Oddly enough, it was easier than I thought possible; he simply asked me during one of our goal setting meetings, "How much money do you want to make this fiscal?" I told him what I thought was a solid number. He laughed in a very encouraging way and said, "You're better than that." I challenged him because I thought the number I had given him was a good number. I remember this moment because a weird emotion hit me when he told me I could do more. It was part anger ("How dare you question me? I already do so much; what can doing more really achieve?" – law of diminishing returns). There was also some fear in there (around maybe I am not as good as I think I am). Honestly, I didn't believe him. I didn't know how to do more than I was or see how doing more would even translate into more. With a very simple question, he shined a light on a blind spot.

What followed was almost a discovery session, similar to what we all put our clients through. Again, we were new to our relationship together, so he sought to understand everything I was doing (he already had some idea) and to get me to explain my process. He learned everything about how I worked and what I did. At the end, as if he already knew the answer, he said, you are good, but you can do more. I simply said, "How?"

Let's take a quick pause here.

I am going to leave you with some important things in this paragraph, and I will get into exactly how to make changes that will forever impact you. More important, you must be coachable. I am not the only person he asked this information from and gave this information to, but I am the one who took the coaching and ran with it. I have always believed that if you want to be the best, you need to be open to learning. You need to be humble, to seek people better than you and to be open to getting a punch of reality. I would argue that the most important thing a salesperson needs to be in their career is coachable.

Ok, let's resume, "How would I double my income?" He told me some obvious stuff. It was clear I needed to prospect more, so he challenged me to figure it out. I needed to up my game by building better business cases, and push executives for data, alignment, validation, and change. This would lead to deeper discovery sessions--discovery that takes twice as long as the presentation to follow. However, most important, he would teach me a new methodology that changed my game forever.

This was called MEDDPICC.

So what do these 8 letters that will forever change your life in sales mean?

METRICS – What is the business case? Think of the hard dollars, real value, and improvements in KPIs that your solution brings that justify a change. This is an actual mathematical equation, not a guess.

ECONOMIC BUYER – Who can spend money, has budget, can CREATE budget, and can sign a contract?

DECISION CRITERIA – What is their wish list? What items will you be measured on and need to achieve to earn their business?

DECISION PROCESS – Who is involved? When do they want to make a decision? When do they want to go live?

PAPER PROCESS – What is the legal process a company will go through? Who are the people involved? How long does it take them to review, redline, and give approval for signature? This is critical to learning to make sure deals close on time.

IDENTIFY PAIN – What are the real issues, goals, and outcomes? This, along with metrics, helps solidify the "Why Change" message.

CHAMPIONS – Who will give you inside information and sell for you when you are not there?

COMPETITION – Who are they? What differentiates you from them? What landmines can you set?

The above criteria are color coded, red, yellow, or green. Your job during the sales process is to get them all to green as fast as possible. Red is information you don't know. Yellow is information you know some of, but it may not be 100% validated. Green means you are 100% confident it is complete and validated by the client.

Now you may be saying to yourself, "David, this stuff is obvious." Yes, yes it is. It was to me when I first saw it, too. However, I went back and applied it to the deals I was working, the ones I had lost, and the ones I had won. Let's just say, my mind was blown. Out of over 50 opportunities across a 20 million dollar pipeline, I didn't win a single deal that still had MEDDPICC criteria still in the red, and all the deals I won had all the criteria in green. Had I known this before, I would have won much more business. Now I challenge you, as I was challenged, pick a deal you are working. Write out the eight letters and be honest with filling in the information. I bet you anything that you have red and yellow all over it. How much is really green?

I will pause here.

Seriously, go do this….I'm waiting…

Now, go do it on the last deal you lost…

Now, go do it on the last deal you won…

You're welcome!

Again, we are all at different stages of our sales development, but this here will change your life. It will show you your blind spots, help you prepare for meetings, and WILL help you win more. It is a race to get these into green faster than your competition. Whoever gets all this information the fastest, and in a complete fashion, will often win. Now, nothing is guaranteed in this world; you could do everything right and still lose. However, using this methodology will increase your chance of winning dramatically.

To wrap this up, seek people who can make you better. (Shout out to Gregory Donovan again here, thanks for everything, Greg! You forever changed my life.) Be coachable, don't be lazy, AND use MEDDPICC.

LET ME KNOW IF ANYTHING CHANGES

By DeJuan Brown

DeJuan Brown cut his teeth in sales at Intuit and currently serves a team as a Regional Sales Manager at Bloomberg BNA. DeJuan was featured in Episode 6 (top1.fm/6). He and his wife are the parents of six kids and DeJuan also contributed two other stories to Volume 1 of *Sales Success Stories*: Why is Why Better Than What and The Janitor Know More Than You

L osing a sale can be devastating, no matter the size of the deal.
I mean the time, effort, and energy we expend to get to the finish line is real.

To get all the way there and not get the deal across impacts so many areas of our lives.

I believe there is a specific type of fatigue that stems from hearing 'thanks for all your time, but we've decided to go another route.'

Several years into my career, my final responses to this rebuff were almost always identical.

I'd often ask the normal, "What made you decide to go that route?" and then finally I'd muster up the strength to utter the dreaded 8-word cliché:

"No problem, **let me know if anything changes.**"

In 5+ years, amazingly, nothing ever changed! At least, not enough changed to prompt a prospect to call me back.

Honestly, I never thought twice about whether my statement would ever even garner a future response.

I was on auto-response when the deal was lost, and being that disconnected from the prospect at the end probably meant that I was disconnected from the beginning.

It wasn't until I started hearing talk about concepts like servant-leadership, service first and customer-centrism that I had an epiphany of some sort.

Well, it was not the kind of epiphany that leads to wholesale change. However, I had enough interest to try some short-term experimentation with these concepts.

The first thing I tried ended up being a game-changer, and I can point to at least three consistent results which persist to this day.

Instead of the dismissive and uncaring "let me know if anything changes," I shifted my focus to what I term the "continuity of service."

I would make helping my prospect my primary goal in my sales meetings. I know many of you are thinking, "DUH!!! What other goals would you have?"

If I'm honest, I had a ton of goals in my meetings during that time. However, at least 90% were singular and self-serving. I wanted the prospect to know all the things my solution could do for them, how long we'd taken to develop these unique features, what other clients were saying about our solution, etc.

Even my discovery process was about "me" and "us"; it was rarely about "them."

'Continuity of service' implied that service had a starting point, but no end. This was the thought that changed the tide.

Listen, I wish I could tell you that I immediately went from 0-100, and I tripled my sales THAT year. It definitely didn't happen that way, so here's the deal.

What changed was my mindset, and therefore my language. Mentally, I went into meetings with the question, "What does service look like for this prospect?"

This question alone meant that I had to ask different questions, listen more completely (complete listening is something I'll address later), and develop a creativity that, up until this point, I'd lacked.

Losing a deal took on an entirely different meaning to me, as I began to think of the loss as yet another opportunity – not a lost opportunity, but an opportunity. My prospect-facing statement of 'let me know if anything changes,' morphed into the internal question. "How can I bring value to this prospect from this point until they either become a client or a source of clients in the future?"

"I'd love it if you'd use me as a resource."

Exchanging one dismissive statement for a veiled call to action, I began to get traction.

Initially, I was deathly afraid that telling folks to use me as a resource would result in a time suck with no real returns attached.

What if every prospect tried to use me for free information, free access to software, or something of the sort? How could I manage requests coming in from every angle while still trying to do my job?

Years later, I've not had such an occurrence and I've seen great results to boot.

Specificity has been key, however. I found that saying, "I'd love it if you'd use me as a resource" alone would leave the prospect without guidance on what that even means.

Once I started unpacking that for them, people would actually take me up on it, see the value in my service and solution, and several times they would boomerang to become clients.

Here's a real and practical example:

After several meetings and a couple of demos, I met with the VP of Tax at a large corporation. I was hoping to get the contract signed that day. All the I's had been dotted and T's crossed, at least in my estimation.

Upon my arrival, we exchange pleasantries and everything was going smoothly. In the midst of this, I state that based on our prior meetings, it seemed natural that we move forward unless there were other questions that had come up.

He looked at me and started, "Well....." Immediately I thought *"Houston, we have a problem."*

The VP began to explain to me his rationale for continuing with their current solution for another year. I let him know the reasons for my disagreement, reiterated to him the value that we'd uncovered during our times together, and ended with the unpacking I referred to earlier.

"I'd love it if you'd use me as a resource. Your team told me that comparative content between the 37 states you do business in is near-impossible to collect efficiently. Based on that, I want to serve you all. I'll send this to the team also, but please let me know when a project requires such a comparative. I'm more than happy to create that chart in real time and send it to you all.

I know that you also periodically deliver time-specific reports to the CFO around developments in the foreign countries you all have interests in. Let me help you there as well. Prior to your next CFO roundtable, let me know the date range you're presenting on, and which jurisdictions you're presenting in. I'll help supplement your research with a summary of all developments from those countries."

The VP now looks at me and says, "Wow, I really appreciate the offer." I look him in the eyes and respond, "No, I'm serious—no strings attached, I'd be excited to serve your organization in this way. If I don't hear from you in a couple weeks, I'll reach out to offer again. In addition, if I come across any content or events that I think would benefit you all, I'll send it your way."

Again, he responded with gratitude.

A week goes by, and I get an email from one of his tax managers that I'd never met with. "DeJuan, Stephen told us that you'd be willing to help us out from time to time. We're actually just starting a project dealing with CTC Reporting, and would like to compare what we're finding to what you guys have." He enumerated the 11 countries in question along with the specific topics, and within 15 minutes, I'd had a comparative chart built and sent over.

Along with that, I sent some special reports and news articles that I knew would matter to them.

A few days later, I get a call from the VP asking me if I'd be willing to come back in and do a demo with their International team. Apparently, the detail of the content I'd sent them went beyond what they could find anywhere else, and they were interested in what it would look like to add our international coverage to their current platform.

Spoiler alert: I went in and demoed to the International team. The response was overwhelming and the VP decided that instead of spending on two platforms, he'd consolidate spend, and simply replace their current solution with our full singular platform.

Service=Sales in this case.

It doesn't always turn out this easily this quickly, that much is true. There have been times that I would've needed to provide valuable content over the course of a year or more in order to acquire a new client.

Nevertheless, the point is three-fold.

1. Service should be the default setting for Sales Professionals.
2. Consistency in service builds value that can't be uncovered during discovery calls nor articulated in a pitch.
3. Commitment to service even after a "loss" is a powerful differentiator.

You may not be in an industry like the one I'm in, so this may look different for you.

Applying the three points above, however, where could you implement this approach in your business?

I LOVE S.A.L.E.S.

By Phil Terrill

Currently, Phil Terrill works on the Global Sales Innovation team at Microsoft on Customer Success Management after having previously been their top Corporate Account Manager. Phil was featured in Episode 39 of the podcast (top1.fm/39) and contributed two other stories to Volume 1 of *Sales Success Stories*: F*@# the Status Quo – Do You, and The Four "F's" to Building the Right Momentum with Customers. He also just released his own self-help book: *Collision Course: 4Fs to Transform Life's Challenges into Powerful Breakthroughs*.

In my previous story, I introduced the 4F Model that helped me transform a dormant customer into a net-new win for Microsoft. However, I left out the story of the journey, effort and long back-and-forth discussion about digital transformation within an industry that was on the brink of severe disruption. Think of this as the "Amazon effect" in which anything that was a brick-and-mortar business needed to rethink how they planned to go to market in the future. At that time, one of my retail customers was really looking at how to evolve their company to match the frictionless way Amazon was targeting their customers. In reality, my customer was trying to figure out how to stay relevant enough for survival. That approach meant revamping their approach to investing in technology. Before I go too far, pay close attention to how I detail out this year-long engagement that developed with a really well-known global retailer in Southern California.

When I met this customer, they were moving down from a higher-tier segment within the company and required significant investment (or they perceived this as required treatment) based on their IT Manager's previous purchase in the region at another global retailer. However, this was my first meeting with the customer and it took a while to get it on the calendar. Let me give you a quick tip – account transitioning from the new fiscal year to the next appears seamless, but it is often the very opposite. In other words, prepare to be surprised by slow processes. Once the account was transitioned, I quickly realized the influence the previous Account Manager had on the customer. My stakeholder was impressed with my ability to get a meeting put together so quickly, given name recognition was part of my territory optimization plan. On the podcast, I referenced being able to "humanize the relationship with technology" and that my first conversations with customers were hardly ever about just tech. My approach was to engage the new contact right where he was, because we actually started at our respective companies around the same time.

Doing critical research on your stakeholders is vital to the long-term success of any seller or person trying to make inroads with a new customer(s). Leverage social media and other platforms to understand your buyer, establish a persona, and feed those interests to ensure you are learning about the person behind the decision maker. When I realized his interests, we connected at varying levels, and this allowed me the opportunity to build a genuine connection. Our mutual interests in dogs, sports, good whiskey and the sun were always talking points. Just imagine if I could talk about LeBron going to the Lakers at that time.

After the connection was developed, I started to focus on providing valuable insights into the industry, access to in-market events, technical resources, and information on new technology that could improve their bottom line for IT (and beyond). The first step was gaining the relationship and now the focus became influence. The better the resource and timeliness of that value, the better off our discussions were about looking at other technology. I was able to steer the conversation towards a full portfolio review, leading to a conversation about how to optimize their investments so as to achieve the same functionality. At this point, it was critical to know my product/solution in order to present immediate value or advice that the customer could review to take action. This moment was critical because I knew that influence was established. We discussed areas they could divest or remove because the investment in a consolidated approach was extremely favorable to the company. In addition, we could reimagine how the company operationalized their retail footprint around the world.

To help the customer reach this destination, my first step was learning about the person who was going to make the decision. Every demo or proof-of-concept (POC) was a brick laid to help us get to the right foundation. My customer had tangible experiences and data at their fingertips to see the possibilities of a revamped technology roadmap. This included closing a three-year net-new deal inked at close to $1.8 million in total value to the customer. While a portion of that value was retired in quota, the impact in helping a customer achieve digital transformation was widely appreciated; the deployment against our roadmap has started making this a huge milestone for my initial stakeholder.

Even with this success, I am sure you are still wondering how this was really completed end-to-end. Well, some of that story is left out because the details might not be cool with Microsoft's legal team. However, I did want you to know what the S.A.L.E.S. acronym is all about, as these were the lessons I learned from collaborating with this retailer as their account executive:

Scale - No one person alone can win the war! Identify who is better than you and utilize their intelligence, expertise, and resources to help your customer(s).

Agility - Create a service level agreement (or SLA) with your customers that is realistic! Customers demand a lot, but you have to set expectations based on what you can actually deliver on time and at scale. There is a partnership that has to be established and **time is a finite resource**. Treat yours and theirs as such!

Leverage - My greatest successes in business, whether sales or not, **directly correlate to leveraging the incredible work and talents of others to create progress**. Progress is defined by business-value solutions, straight-forward results, and an undeniable appetite for excellence. The team won with our customers, because of leveraging each other in our best ways to be successful!

Experience - The best teacher of them all! **The only way to get results is to have skin in the game and just go for it**. Otherwise, you might as well go do something else with your time. Michael Jordan said, "I can accept failure, but I cannot accept not trying" and that is an excellent perspective from arguably the greatest to ever do it in any sport!

Sacrifice - Success is about failing so fast that your next success makes you forget you ever failed in the first place. You have to be willing to go beyond the status quo for your customers! Bring them on the journey with you and it will be a different experience. Show them you are willing and able, but do it in a manner that exudes excellence. Be healthy and balanced in the process - no sale is worth dying over. Trust me on that one! Make that one extra call or type that one last email to a customer in order to increase the chances! The best are great because they do that little bit more than the others. **Greatness is a state of mind and not just a destination!**

The S.A.L.E.S. acronym is a framework that I still consider in my actions, as it provides key objectives or skills that I should constantly be driving towards with customers and partners. I hope you are able to utilize the stories to help you reach the 1% of performers. See you at the top!

YOU CAN HAVE EVERYTHING

By Leila Mozaffarian

Leila Mozaffarian is a Senior Account Executive at Zipwhip in Seattle. She was their top performer in 2017 and remained within the top performers in 2018. Leila was featured in Episode 50 of the *Sales Success Stories* Podcast (top1.fm/50) She is working on two other stories for Volume 2 of *Sales Success Stories*: Create a 5 Star Experience for Your Customers & Don't Put All Your Eggs in One Basket

When I was little girl, I was told by my parents, teachers, mentors, etc. that you can do anything you set your mind to. While I didn't go into the WNBA, I did learn a very important life lesson and have always made sure to keep this concept in my mind. YOU CAN HAVE EVERYTHING.

You can have everything, but you can't always have it at the same time. In life and in sales, some things are obviously outside of our control, but the majority of the basics are in our complete control. When it comes to sales, "controlling the controllables" is key. Without doing so, it is very hard to become a top performer and especially to be a consistent top performer. This is not a natural talent and there is no easy secret. Anyone can learn to work hard and take control – it is all about the mindset!

When did I achieve this mindset? When did I believe that I can have everything?

Well, growing up I spent a lot of time in the hospital for different family emergencies. As a middle school student, my parents taught me at a young age to keep up with my school work and extracurriculars regardless of what obstacles were thrown my way. There were no excuses. I controlled my time and effort in my work.

Fast forward to June 2016: I had just graduated from the University of Oregon. I wanted my first job to be at a tech startup that gave me the opportunity to learn how to handle all aspects of the business so I could learn, fail, and grow. Little did I know, Zipwhip was going to be where I created a family at work who supported me in every way from a business and personal aspect.

When I first started in July 2016, I came into sales without knowing that the stereotypical salesperson was a white man with experience – at least in my direct customer base. I was a young woman, with no sales experience, and a Persian background. My specific target market was within the automotive industry (let's be honest – older, white, men who were oftentimes born into the automotive family). This was very difficult for me at first – I felt underprepared, I felt like I had more obstacles to handle, and I didn't know how this was going to play out. What if I failed? What if I was not able to learn how to sell innovative software (a business text messaging tool to existing business phone numbers) to folks who don't really focus on being "high tech" when it comes to their communications? What if I didn't hit my quota? What if I was the worst sales rep?

In the back of my mind. I thought: "I have control over the basics. I can learn. I can succeed." Let's be honest though - in the front of my mind, I thought: "You are GOING TO FAIL."

At the time, Zipwhip's business model was the entire cycle: make your own leads, set your own meetings, complete the demos, generate new sales, train and support your customers, manage your own book of business based off of your sales, and continue this cycle month after month.

We had a four-month ramp period. I hit my goals and requirements at a steady rate in my first four months. In January 2017, when I was on my full ramp for sales, I missed a quota. How could you miss? Why did you miss? Lack of effort? Needed more dials? Got too comfortable? Dried out your pipeline? What had I done?

Now to provide you with some perspective on my personal life at the time – January 9th, 2017 was one of the worst days of my life. I broke up with my partner of five and a half years. That evening, I found out that my grandmother was diagnosed with cancer. It was a lot. I was broken in many ways. I couldn't control what was happening. A few weeks later, my father was diagnosed with an incurable disease. Weeks later, I received a call that my mother had been hit by a tow truck and her car was totaled. I HAD NO CONTROL. I felt like I had the lost the game; I felt like my life was all coming to an end. I was trying to figure out how to handle everything at once as one of the primary caregivers for both my grandmother, father, and focusing on not only my first but relatively new job.

Everyone goes through hardships – no one person has it better than anyone else, and we all have our own baggage and handle pressures in our own way. I could not fix what was happening. I could not cure diseases, I could not stop a car accident that had already happened, and sadly, I was very angry at the situation. What happened to no excuses? What happened to just working hard and seeing results? What happened to never being too busy?

Before we get too dark – this story does have a happy ending. I may not have had it all on a personal level but this entire experience allowed me to have everything I wanted on a career level.

At this point, I could only control a few things, and so I made a list:

1. You know your time is limited, so spend time with your family.

2. Your parents aren't working now.... these types of medical expenses are expensive – make money!

3. You have control of how much you make and how quickly you make it – make money!

I felt like I only had control of one aspect of my life – my job. How could I succeed and what could I control? I could control how many calls I made, how many emails I sent, and how many hours I worked. In February 2017, I put my heart and soul into the work I was doing. I went out of my way to learn about all the sub verticals in the automotive industry and the business model behind each department (i.e. service, sales, parts, BDC). I had different applications I signed up for that would notify me of big automotive company changes, send me newsletters, and I read B2B magazines focused within the automotive space. I had to appear as knowledgeable about the industry as the gentleman who was basically born into the automotive world. I had to prove myself to them if I was to earn their trust, respect, and business. I had to learn about salespeople who really knew how to sell.

After work I would read books on anything I could (i.e startups, tech companies, cold calls), I listened to podcasts, I interviewed thought leaders I found on LinkedIn, and I did anything else I could think of to just learn.

In March 2017, I had one of the best months and I know my mentors and leaders at the company were amazed. At the time, Zipwhip did not have a full support or marketing team. I had studied marketing in college so I tried to get creative – making infographics based off of what seemed to be successful online. I used LinkedIn a lot to try and connect with business industry experts. I did what the average salesperson is not told to do.

After achieving a very successful month and knowing whether I could help to support my family, I knew that I had to do it again. I continued exceeding expectations by a lot. I built better relationships with our C-level team and constantly asked them to help guide me in the right direction as we were growing exponentially. I was creating a name and career for myself and creating a name for Zipwhip.

In June 2017, I reflected and noticed that a lot had happened in six months:

1. I had three consecutive months that shocked many people due to the amount of business I had generated and the turn-around time in creating that new business.

2. I had set the highest software sales record at the company.

3. I was asked to write in multiple magazines and articles TO PEOPLE IN THE AUTOMOTIVE SPACE!! I was becoming an influencer.

4. I got promoted internally at Zipwhip, feeling as though I had earned the respect and recognition for myself.

5. I was pushing salespeople who had been there longer than me to see and believe even more in what Zipwhip and what we were capable of doing.

At one point, my personal expectation was to be number one both on a monthly basis and for the year. Now bear in mind that my ENTIRE motivation was my family. I could control telling my father to not worry about treatment, to help my mom figure out her car situation, to help my grandmother pay her finances. Sales allowed me to have "everything" I wanted.

I had a lot of people doubt my success. I was told that I was lucky and that it "wouldn't last long term". This crushed me – but more so, it motivated me to prove the people around me wrong even more. I had so much going on at home, but I had to remember that I had control over my job. At the end of December 2017, when it was officially announced that I was number one for the year, I was ecstatic. I had what I considered "everything" – my family, my performance at work in both sales and growth opportunity, and my happiness.

In January 2018, I was promoted again and I took on the highest level of quota attainment through a new model we had put in place. I was hitting my numbers and things were going smoothly for the first quarter or so. In April 2018, things took a big turn for my father. We spent about a month in the hospital and we were not sure if he was going to make it home. I had to work with the situation and not against it. During his resting hours, I would run into the lobby or café and do demos remotely with businesses across the country. Every single day was a battle. Was today the day that he would be gone? Do I spend more time in the room with him or do I focus on making money? What if he does come home and we need financial backing?

While I was not following my normal prospecting routine, I had built incredible relationships with my customers. Side note – do that, ALWAYS take care of your customers. Provide them with a five-star experience and make sure you give them a reason to vouch for you.

Let me give you a brief example of how they make the biggest difference. On the last day of April 2018, I was sitting in the ICU and looking out at Lake Washington. I needed one more deal to hit my quota. There were 10-15 doctors in the room giving us advice on what to do about my father. I texted my current customer, asked for a referral, and he practically sold it for me. Within one hour, I had hit my quota.

After a few weeks at the hospital, my father was getting sent home! Yet another miracle.

For the last eight months at home, I had many sleepless nights and self-care has not been a priority to me. I sent emails at all hours of the night and had the most random routine – which as many of you know, is not helpful when it comes to sales. Nonetheless, I have control of what to do with my family now, how to handle my customers, and how to maintain success.

We are now at the end of 2018. I am proud to say that my father and my grandmother have fought through everything that has been thrown at them and we celebrated entering 2019 together. I am also proud to say that I still was able to be in the top 10 of our sales team while being out for so much of the year.

My point to all of this? You can control your sales experience. Put the time and effort and hours in that those around you may not and work your way up. Have faith in yourself, no matter what life throws at you. Do not create reasons for your failures; but also know that every "successful" person has failed.

My challenge to you? Write down what you can control based off what you want. Create a plan and go after it! You really can have everything but again, maybe just not all at once.

MY GREATEST WIN
AT MICROSOFT

By Carson Heady

Carson Heady is a top sales performer and cloud transformation specialist at Microsoft. He spoke with Scott in Episode 54 of the podcast (top1.fm/54) and is working on two other stories for Volume 2 of *Sales Success Stories*: How Deal Transparency Turned a Bad Situation Into a Substantial Upsell & How Networking and Social Selling Created a Unique, Global Deal. He is also the author of the Birth of a Salesman Trilogy.

My greatest win at Microsoft – personally and professionally – was one that occurred solely because of using tools at my disposal, prospecting heavily with social selling, and building a strong relationship once I had opened that initial door.

Thanks to reports we had access to which detailed customer consumption in efforts to try or test cloud services, I was able to find a handful of clients that were testing at enough velocity that it certainly warranted a conversation – how could we help? What were they trying to do? Was it a competitive situation? From there, I could utilize LinkedIn (full disclosure: Microsoft purchased LinkedIn, so this is not an endorsement) to find the organizations and people to connect with at the company. I cast a wide net to maximize response, so for this particular organization, I targeted roughly 30 folks in various stakeholder positions (C-Suite, VP, and IT/innovation) and the numbers game soon kicked in. Of those 30, 11 accepted my invitation to connect and only 1 responded to my subsequent e-mail about why I had reached out and how I could help with resources. He told me who I needed to talk to (another person entirely that I had not already connected with) so I reached out.

The outreach needs to be personal but also unique – it was a smaller organization and start-up, so they were initially shocked to hear from my company. Second – I was not looking to sell anything. My outreach was targeted toward inquiring about their needs and usage and about different incentives and programs we may have to help them further explore or scope out the desired solution. That outreach was designed to set a meeting; the meeting was set.

In my mind, from my experience, I had a pre-conceived notion that this may be a relatively smaller deal with the opportunity to grow, but I never let that thought inform my actions. Setting the meeting with the right business decision maker is the most important first piece of the process and once I was in the room, across the table it was all about establishing the relationship.

I effectively positioned myself as an advocate for this client – one who could absolutely utilize my assistance and that of my organization. Through needs analysis, we discovered that there was a number of potential opportunities to expand as these folks were ambitious but just really starting their exploration of a cloud journey. Their industry is exciting and the possibilities of how data could be monetized were endless. The conversation touched on areas of challenge for them regarding existing infrastructure. While they were merely testing our platform for an unrelated reason, we brought in proper resources and partners and relatively quickly moved their infrastructure to our platform. They became my largest-consuming account for an entire year, despite being a fraction of the size of several other large organizations.

Fast forward about a year. The projects there had multiplied and the organization was now getting quite a bit of love and attention from Microsoft. I had been able to set up conversations with a half-dozen different facets of our organization based on desires they had or additional resources/benefits that existed and would enhance the relationship. In short, I brought every bit of value I could to their team.

That said, the company was positioning itself to be purchased, and this purchase did indeed transpire, throwing a lot of current projects up in the air.

The day the purchase transpired, I was able to successfully find the new parent company and subsidiaries, as well as virtually connect to the new CEO, CIO, and CFO. I was in the office of the new CIO the following week, and our conversations generated an additional multi-million dollar pipeline.

The conversations would not have existed without social selling. The social selling would not have been successful without using a litany of different methods of connecting or targeting a large number of individuals with unique, impactful scripting. The relationship never would have worked without adding value and resources and serving as advocate every step of the way, never worrying about the sale or dollar amounts.

After the company purchase, I was successful in landing additional projects at the new company, was able to liaise with people I connected with at that company who went to other companies post-buyout (the relationships continued, often times equating to new projects with different organizations) and received a substantial amount of attention internally as my prospecting methods were highlighted in a podcast by the Vice President of Microsoft United States.

TAKING ON A NEW CHALLENGE

By Jeremy Leveille

Jeremy Leveille is LeadIQ's top SDR and Sales Development Lead. He was featured in episode 55 of the podcast (top1.fm/55) and has written two other stories for Volume 2 of *Sales Success Stories*: Dad Jokes and Direct Mail for the Win.

I was a BDR (Business Development Representative) at a mid-market technology company. I was doing really well, exceeding quota for meetings set for nine months in a row. One month I even hit 246% to quota. At this time, I was starting to post content on LinkedIn and build my personal brand. Recruiters took notice and started knocking on my door.

I was happy at my current company but I was open to see if there was anything else I could do. I was offered a role as a BDR Team Leader at another company. I accepted the offer, but after letting my current company know that I was leaving they made a counter-offer/promotion.

After much deliberation, I accepted the counter-offer/promotion to stay at my company as a Channel Sales Manager.

This change was exciting but also nerve-racking at the same time. After all, I barely had any experience in a closing role and new very little about what being a Channel Sales Manager (a.k.a. Channel Manager) was like. Adding to the anxiety was the fact that the person who would be my manager had just left the company so the person who I'd be reporting to was located five states away and had a full plate of traveling all over the country to manage other reps.

Despite the obstacles, I was determined to succeed in this new role. Right off the bat, there was a big event in my area - lots of the important people I'd be working with at my new role were going to be there. The event was put on by Telarus, one of our larger partners. My manager wasn't sure if I was ready to go, but I insisted. I went and although I did feel a little more overwhelmed about not having enough expertise in this new role, I did feel better about making so many great connections.

After that event, I was more eager than ever to continue to learn about how I could succeed in this new role. As I soon discovered, the IT/telecom partner channel is a much different world than direct sales. It's very niche with lots of intricacies. I started networking on LinkedIn with more and more people from the channel, and I found out about a podcast called "Channel Outlaws" through LinkedIn.

This podcast was the absolute game-changer for me in this role. I was able to learn all of the nuances of the channel. Everything I wanted to learn was here. I was hooked and listened to literally every second of every the first 20 episodes (they're an hour long each). Just like that, I now was an expert in my new role. This were all finally starting to click, I was feeling more comfortable in the role. I had a full list of partners I could call my own and had closed my first couple of deals.

When things really took off for me as a Channel Manager, I started to use video. The reason is that a big part of my job was training our reseller and referral partners on the value of our services, what our core products were, what types of deals to refer us, how we differed from the competition, etc. In other words, I had to train our partners on how to sell our stuff. While I would go to the partners' office or hop on a conference call to do these training sessions, traveling around isn't scalable and it's not easy to get groups of people to all be available at the same time for meetings.

As a result, I started recording customized videos myself using a tool called Vidyard. I made a bunch of these videos, some were customized to the specific partner I was sending them to, some were customized based on a particular product. I sent them to partners via email, so they could watch them at whatever time was convenient for them. I was blown away by the response that I was getting!

Not only were the partners super impressed by how thorough the training videos were (thanks to my hours of studying my craft via the podcast), but they also liked the convenience of being able to watch the videos whenever they wanted as opposed to having to shift things around in their busy schedule for a meeting. The biggest reason I think they were such a hit was that it was something that literally no other Channel Manager - at my company or any other - was doing. It was different, and embedding personalized videos into emails for sales was really starting to take off at the time.

The best part was what happened next. A package arrived in the mail at our head office with my name on it. It was from Telarus. Inside was a Telarus Coin of Excellence and a handwritten letter from our liaison at Telarus. The Coin of Excellence (pictured below) is a gold coin that they only present to a select few people who are affiliated with their company (Channel Managers and sales agents) who truly go above and beyond to help make their company a success.

I was working with many partners who were affiliated with Telarus, and in all the communications, I made sure to copy my Liaison there. She said in the letter how appreciative she was for me keeping her in the loop as well as how impressed she was with the videos I had been sending out to her partners.

I was on cloud nine after that. The next month I closed the biggest deal of my sales career.

The biggest takeaways here:

- Don't be afraid of a new challenge - dive in head first!
- Find whatever podcast will arm you with the most expertise in your role - absorb it
- Use video to break through the noise
- Don't be afraid to do something that's different than what everyone else in your role is doing - especially if it's something that is a more practical way of doing your job

HOLD ON – YOU'RE ON AN UNSTOPPABLE ROLLERCOASTER

By Abel Lomas

Abel Lomas is the top Account Executive at TrustRadius. He shared his story with Scott in Episode 59 of the podcast (top1.fm/59) and is working on two other stories for Volume 2 of *Sales Success Stories*: Hong Kong, Singapore, Toronto, Philippines and more: International Selling from the "Cloffice" & Keeping Prospects in Suspense Can Be a Great Tactic, but Show Up to the Sales Call.

Selling Like You're Speed Dating

When I started in my new role at a ~50 person start-up in April of 2018, I had a few set target accounts that I absolutely wanted to win. Think of this as the shortlist that's more important than the commission check. It's about something bigger – an account that I wanted to secure as part of my tenure with the company.

To no surprise, the BDR team had been hammering the account for months with no response. I joined in the fun and three of us were targeting the account. Then, just a couple weeks later, a VP of Marketing from the target account registered on our site and we had a meeting scheduled for May 21st.

The meeting was like a speed date that went all too well. We quickly escalated to a proposal on May 24th, then to price/package negotiations, then to starting the contract redline process on June 1st with a target to have a contract signed by mid-June. We had done a couple rounds of redlines and had 1 open redline item when the account went silent. It wasn't until June 26th when we finally heard back, indicating that the contract was on hold until mid-July. As most teams do, we tried multiple "hero" outreaches including executive-to-executive level outreaches, all of which were ignored. We wouldn't be closing the deal within the calendar quarter, and to make the emotional state even worse, on June 28th another vendor in our space tweeted about their relationship with the company which included a quote from the company's CMO.

From Dead to A Renewed Chase

As the calendar flipped to July, I advised my leadership team that one of three things would happen.

1. We'd be awarded the business as negotiated in Q3 (unlikely)

2. We'd have to renegotiate and settle for a smaller deal (possible) - or worst case -

3. The deal was actually dead and we'd have to start from scratch (most likely)

On July 17, as we attempted to re-engage, what we were already thinking was finally confirmed – the deal was dead and they subsequently wouldn't revisit a partnership until 2019.

It may be all business and not personal, but I took this personally. I started the grieving process with sadness, reflection, and thought. My stomach was twisted in knots as I reflected on the situation. I examined every step and every action I had taken. Also, by the Friday of that week, I came to the conclusion that I hadn't "sold" the account and I needed to reset my frame of mind and start a new pursuit. I was hungry, and my mind was now free to think of new possibilities.

Saturday morning began full of excitement. While the CMO had previously alluded us, I had a plan to finally get him engaged. Whether true or not, the reason I heard why the project was stalled was due to a soft Q2. As a result, my plan was to text him at noon ET on Saturday, knowing that he wouldn't be in a business meeting. Here is how that played out, with the names removed:

July 21, 2018, 12:02 ET

> <CMO name>, If you truly believe your buyers trust your customers before your marketing, we should discuss how to make <your company> truly customer powered to prevent another disappointing quarter. You don't have to buy (now), but accept my challenge and let's share vision.

July 21, 2018, 12:24 ET

> Hi Abel appreciate the enthusiasm... full transparency we don't have any budget until January to do anything comprehensive with you, but looking forward to chatting.

With just a few lines of text on a cell phone, the chase is reborn, and the chase was real. It took until August 16 to have my first meeting with the new VP of Marketing. She brought several people to the table, all of whom deferred to her in the meeting. Within one breath, it was clear that she has a high IQ and is extremely kind but won't hesitate to be extremely direct. It was clear that she had the respect and attention of everyone, whether on this call or anywhere she was present. The call went well, yet she didn't show up for our next call on September 4th. She also wouldn't accept the rescheduled date for September 12th, so I texted her early that morning when I thought she might be between the train and her office. She responds with the following message:

Abel: Adding <name> who is my new VP of Marketing – she's leading the charge. I'll let the two of your connect from here.

The call itself was turned into a discussion about the business justification. I told her how we approach business justification and she shared with me what she needed in the justification. By Wednesday, September 19th, the justification was in her inbox. I asked her for the opportunity to review together, to which she responded that she'd get back to me next week. With her not willing to commit time, we planned a trip to see her in person. We built a whole itinerary around meeting her without knowing if she'd even show up. With this in mind, we de-risked the trip in two different ways:

1. We scheduled meetings with several other companies to make good use of the trip

2. We worked with a champion within this account to block out time when the VP of Marketing was likely to be available

Fast forwarding to Oct 4th, we were on the ground in NYC. That morning was just beautiful. Mild yet cool, clear skies, and NYC was bustling with its usual energy. That morning our primary reason for the trip – meeting with the VP of Marketing – had finally accepted our meeting invitation.

The Face to Face

Later that afternoon, we arrived in the office lobby and rode up the elevator to their floor. We were greeted by three friendly souls at the reception desk who signed us in and showed us to the water cooler. They had us take a seat as we waited for the VP of Marketing to come to get us. If we planned this right, this would be her last meeting of the day and we expected her to be late with the hope that she wouldn't be in a rush to see us off. About 15 minutes after the planned start time, she comes out to greet us. She first introduces herself to my boss and they shake hands. Second, she turns to me with her hand extended to which I told her I was going to need a hug. In fairness, I created an awkward moment and got an awkward side hug. We then turn as she led us to a large, high-tech conference room overlooking a massive screen. She asked us if we wanted to plug in to present but we declined to have a conversation instead (although I had every piece of content possible ready if necessary).

We started the meeting by finding common ground in people we knew in common and finding some commonly shared experiences. It took no time to realize that this was truly a magnificent person we were sitting across from. After only about 10 minutes, and before getting into any prepared content, she pauses the meeting and proceeds to tell us that she likes us personally and respected our commitment to not just the hard work we put into every meeting, but by delivering value to her and her team at every touchpoint in the buyer journey with us. Even though she didn't have this in her budget plan, she wanted to put together a deal.

Her next question... What is the smallest deal we can do just to get started? After answering her question, I finally shared what she didn't know. I told her that we had negotiated a deal in May and we were just a week away from signing when the deal went on hold. Her reaction was priceless, "Abel! If I had known how we screwed you I would have been more empathetic to you. Tell me what that deal was and let's get it done." Now, maybe she would have been empathetic if I had told her sooner, but to this day I believe that I had to earn that moment of empathy. If I had shared that information any sooner, I wouldn't have gotten the reaction I received that day.

As we prepared to depart her office, she once again greeted my boss with a handshake. She then turns to me with her arms open and says, "Abel, bring it in." As we exited the elevator and exited the building back into the streets of NYC, we were greeted with the chill of a cold fall downpour. There is no other way to say this, but we had made it rain.

A few weeks later on Oct 31st, we officially added this new fantastic customer. Had we followed the typical path, we might just be restarting the sales cycle now. Also, maybe by 2020, I could call them a customer. Instead, we challenged each other and ended up deciding that a partnership was worth more than waiting for fiscal budgets to work themselves out.

Lessons Learned

1. Sales might be a rollercoaster, but it is the REP that needs to be UNSTOPPABLE. Otherwise, the rollercoaster is likely to stop at the wrong point in the buyer journey.

2. Deliver value at every touchpoint, whether on a scheduled call, a note between meetings, or any other time that a customer is touched. VALUE TRUMPS AVAILABLE BUDGET.

3. If you don't have a clear state of mind, do what it takes to achieve clarity before you act. The result of a CLEAR MIND will make all the difference in the world.

4. We all know about the Challenger Sale, but challenge everything including yourself, your team, your prospects, their boss(es), and your customers. If there is no challenge, it's not worth the fight.

5. Be HUMAN. Show EMPATHY and practice empathy in every customer touchpoint. Some people might call it karma, but you never know when the empathy will be turned in your favor.

THE REAL VALUE ADD IN SALES

By Jack Wilson

Jack Wilson left his top 1% level performance as a business banking relationship manager at Citizens Bank for his current role as the Director of Business Development at Cinch IT. You can hear Jack's story in episode 57 of the podcast (top1.fm/57). Jack is working on two other stories for Volume 2 of Sales Success Stories: Don't step on your own Bananas & Setting Your Success on Auto Pilot

Value-add. In my opinion, this is one of the most misused terms in sales. With the explosion of the inside sales role over the past few years, the term has become a battle cry for those who adopt a regular cadence or pattern of outreach. Never "touch base" or "check-in"; always ensure that you're providing "value-added contacts". While the former is great advice, the latter is often applied with reckless abandon in regards to what "Value" really means or, more importantly, who perceives that value.

So what is value?

Val-ue: noun: The regard that something is held to deserve; the importance, worth, or usefulness of something.

That's what the dictionary says value means, but it's easy to forget that much like beauty, value is in the eye of the beholder. In sales, the beholder is our prospect. You're probably thinking "no kidding." Nonetheless, if it's that obvious, why do most salespeople fail to consider this when preparing their so-called value-added contacts?

As a leader in Business Development, I receive countless e-mails from sales reps that want to sell me lead generation tools. It's not uncommon for those e-mails to include facts about why lead generation is so critical to a business or to contain links to industry articles that highlight the use case for similar tools. To those, I return the favor and say "No kidding!" If I'm in a sales leadership position and I don't understand why generating new leads is important, then I have bigger issues that need to be addressed. Although that information is important, which is a key component to the definition of value, is it useful? I would argue that important information is fairly well known and if, as the prospect, I already know then how is it useful to me. What value are you adding?

Sun Tzu once said, "To hear the sound of Thunder is no sign of a quick ear." In other words, don't be captain obvious. If something is important then a business leader should and most likely will be well aware of it. The REAL value comes into play when something you share, do, or recommend is USEFUL. Something has value when it's useful in a way that someone can adopt it, learn it, or use it to have an impact on their goals.

My story is one about adding tangible value to a prospect in order to win over their business. The year was 2014, and I was the better part of a year into my career as a Business Banking Relationship Manager. That's a fancy title for someone who brings in new business customers to the bank. I had recently notched a few good wins with businesses in the plastics distribution industry. Through my experiences with these clients, I became somewhat of an authority in their line of business. I used this expertise to hyper-focus myself on prospecting into that vertical. I was able to land appointments with relative ease because I was developing an understanding of the one or two biggest pains they experience and tailoring my message to those specific points.

The very first prospect I called using this approach gave me the typical "I'm all set" when I first called, but that's when I said very deliberately "I'm not calling you out of happenstance; I'm calling because every time I've worked with a polymer distributor they've struggled to have the means necessary to purchase bulk loads of unique materials because they lack the available capital... does that happen to you often?" To this, the prospect responded: "Now you're speaking my language, as a matter of fact, it does. There's not much we can do about it though" he said. "That's just the nature of our business."

Insert value here!

This is the point when I delivered real value. I explained to the prospect a real-world example of how I solved that problem for a client of mine and reinforced it by letting him know it wasn't a onetime gig and that I have several examples available as a reference if he would like to discuss it further. Needless to say, I booked the appointment.

What happened over the next TWO YEARS was one of the most rewarding and eye-opening experiences of my career. You read it right – I said two years. Obviously you never want your sales cycle to be this long but far too often sales professionals will cut and run if they can't see the finish line.

This prospect was different. Upon initial discovery, the business fit all the criteria of an ideal client. They were the right revenue size. They were in the right industry. They already utilized many of the services we were proposing to them. So what was the hold-up? Working for a bank is different than most types of sales in that the opportunity doesn't close with a signature. A business can open an account with you any time, but what happens if they need a loan or a line of credit and their application gets declined? Well, that's the situation we found ourselves in, and it was a deal breaker.

In most situations, I would have looked at this scenario like any other rejection. I would have chalked it up as one in the loss column and kept moving on, yet I developed a bond with this prospect. I had invested so much of my time learning about the industry and targeting my prospecting efforts. Even more so, I had truly gained a deeper understanding of this particular business and I understood overwhelmingly how my solution would impact them in a positive manner. So I went all in. I asked myself: "how I can help steer their business in the right direction?"

Instead of walking away from the opportunity with a simple "I'm sorry," I sat with them at a follow-up meeting and explained in as detailed a manner as I could why they were not eligible for the loan. I then took it one step further. I highlighted a few key areas in their financials that If improved would most likely result in an approval. Before the meeting ended, we not only established several metrics to improve, but we also outlined actual strategies that they could employ in order to reach their goals. Lastly, I made a commitment to follow up with them regularly, acting as an accountability partner of sorts.

One month later, I made my first follow-up call. I think I was as surprised by their reaction to my call, as they were at the fact that I had actually followed through and called. Being used to every other vendor, banker, and salesperson, they made the assumption that they would likely never hear from me again. I didn't call to "check in" or "touch base"; instead I called with a purpose. I asked about the milestones we had set and how they were making progress toward them. Over the next several months, I scheduled regular follow-ups. Finally, a little under a year later, they called me. "We've got great news, I think we're ready," they told me. We scheduled a meeting to collect all the documents and although they hadn't quite achieved all of their milestones, it was close. So we gave it another shot.

......Declined!

I thought that was it – the trust would be broken. The faith they had in my advice and guidance was lost. Still, I was wrong again. Three weeks later, I received a called from the prospect's bookkeeper. She told me that she knew I was due to call them in another week's time, but they really needed my advice. Sadly, I didn't have a scheduled follow-up this time. I had given up. I thought to myself, why I have wasted so much time for one opportunity. The prospect had become so accustomed to my follow-ups though, that they beat me to it. It was then that I realized I had earned the trusted advisor status sales professionals seek with all of their prospects and clients. I didn't schedule another follow-up call with this prospect, but like clockwork, they would reach out every month or so to ask me how certain decisions might impact their goal of becoming a lendable business.

Then one day I received a call from the prospect asking for a meeting. The date was almost two years to the day from when I had first prospected them. When I arrived at their office, they had compiled a complete package for another attempt at a loan application. I had to do almost nothing; it was the most complete package I had received in a while. Even more impressive were their metrics. The business had essentially transformed itself into a leaner meaner more efficient operation. We submitted the application and the loan was approved.

The transformation that followed was incredible. The business has since doubled its annual revenue, they've expanded into a larger facility and have even hired over a dozen new employees. The most incredible part is that none of that is because of the loan. It took some real deep reflection to understand that the advice and guidance I had given them originated from the desire to earn their business, but beyond earning their business I had provided real value. It's not the kind of value you send in an e-mail or post in an article. I had provided them with actionable ideas that helped to transform their business forever. There isn't much more rewarding of a feeling. The five additional clients they referred me to that would become customers certainly felt good nonetheless.

Lessons Learned:

- When making "value-added contacts," don't be captain obvious

- Use your experiences to become an expert in an industry
- Use your expert status to speak deliberately to your prospects in order to get their attention
- Have skin in the game and take pride in bringing your solution to a prospect or client
- Develop a systematic method for follow-up and stick to it
- Provide real, tangible value that a prospect can use to impact their business at every opportunity

HOW I BEAT OUT 300 CANDIDATES FOR MY DREAM SALES JOB

By Scott Barker

Scott Barker is Head of Partnerships at Sales Hacker which was recently acquired by Outreach.io. Scott was featured in episode 53 of the podcast (top1.fm/53) and is working on two other stories for Volume 2 of *Sales Success Stories*: How to Close $2M in Your First Year on the Job & How to Successfully Navigate an Acquisition.

Beating out the competition to land a sales job is hard. Beating out 300 applicants for your dream job can seem nearly impossible. However, every amazing experience that I've had thus far in my career has been somewhere on the other side of "impossible." In this story, I'm going to share with you how I was able to cross the seemingly impossible chasm and land my dream job:

I loved my job. I was 24 years old, a business development manager at a fast-growing SAAS startup, I had hired a team full of close friends & we were all crushing it. I really had no intentions of going anywhere, but sometimes opportunities are put in front of you that are too good to pass up. A company that I had been following for a long time, Sales Hacker, was looking for a new head of partnerships; I immediately knew I had to throw my hat in the ring. The network I would gain would act as a springboard for my career, so I got tunnel vision and went to work.

The problem? 300 other sales professionals were also gunning for this job and many of them worked at Tier 1 tech companies like Salesforce, DocuSign, and Adobe, possessing way more experience and educations at fancy business schools like Duke, Stanford or Columbia. So how did I manage to tumble out the other side of the hiring process?

Here is my step by step process for landing any sales job:

1. **Always Be Connecting**: The work starts before you ever even find your "dream job." You have to be constantly net-working as a sales professional so that you're in the know of upcoming openings. Make sure that your LinkedIn profile is crisp at all times. You never know who could be looking! In my particular case, the only announcement was a Linke-dIn post, so if I wasn't part of the CEO's network, I never would have even known about this opportunity.

2. **Follow a Process**: Reframe your mind to start looking at the hiring process as you would your sales process. In my case, I told the hiring manager straight away that I was going to do my best to go through this process as I would with one of their partners. If you're not rock-solid on this process, which is arguably the most important sales process you'll ever run with them, then how can they expect you to rock it with their clients? For me, In order to apply, you had to complete a Google form with 8 questions. I made sure that I had thoughtful answers & bugged a friend to proofread for me. Attention to details & speed of responsiveness matter - don't shoot yourself in the foot before you begin!

3. **Engage Multiple Stakeholders**: Now it's time to engage other stakeholders and find yourself a champion! I reached out to the person currently in the role & another person in the C-suite. Try to set up a zoom call (video on), lead with curiosity, and position it as you wanting to make sure that it's a perfect fit for both parties. This is the perfect time to showcase that you're a good culture fit that and that you're someone they'd want to work with every day. I was able to make a strong connection with the VP of Marketing, who would act as my champion throughout (shoutout to Gaetano DiNardi).

4. **Take an Omni-channel Approach**: I made sure that the hiring manager (in this case it was the CEO, Max Altschuler) knew who I was - I went all in on email, LinkedIn, Twitter, and Instagram. Think you're being too pushy? I'll tell you right now, you're not. Maybe if you were going for an engineering role but this is sales, persistence is good.

5. **Be Passionate & Prepared**: After all that, I was given the opportunity to jump on a phone interview. I was pretty nervous, so I tried to focus on the things I could control. In this case, I knew that even if I was the smoothest, I could certainly be the most passionate and prepared. I came to the interview with an agenda, I knew their TAM, I had a 30-60-90 plan, I knew their offering through and through, had some suggestions/tweaks they could possibly make, had a list of answers (or stories) for common questions and of course had some intelligent questions of my own prepared. Make sure that you always get concrete next steps!

6. **Send a Video Follow-up**: As soon as the interview wraps up, make sure that you're following up, thanking them for their time, and reiterating how excited you are about the opportunity. In my case, I sent a quick video instead of just a normal email to try to further separate myself from the pack.

7. **Stay Busy**: Now, at this point, most people play the waiting game. However, you must ask yourself, just like a sales

process, is there anything that I could be doing that would increase my chances of getting to the next round? For me, it was staying active on their social channels with thoughtful comments and looping in with my champion to do a quick debrief on the interview.

8. **Always Get Next Steps**: Now for the real interview: I was on to the next round which was your classic longer, more formal video interview. At this point, I started to let myself hope that there was a chance so I doubled down & made sure I had my best success stories down pat. At this point, my main goal was to explain exactly how I'd get us to where we need to be while showing how passionate I was about the organization. You need to show that you're not just looking for a job, you're looking for THIS job. Of course, try to close the next steps and ask if there is anything they can see that would stop you from getting the job.

9. **Go Above & Beyond**: I'm overly critical of myself, so I left this interview thinking that I didn't hit on a number of points that I had hoped to bring up. Luckily, I was told the next day that I made the shortlist: it was me and one other person. I don't think I slept for two days…but once again, I asked myself "is there anything I could do right now to improve my chances?" I decided that there was! So I ended up hiring a graphic designer to help me build a sales deck on "Why I was perfect for the Job," I even included quotes from all of my past bosses in there.

10. **Do A Hiring Review** (like a deal review): I got a phone call the next day from the CEO saying that although it had been a ridiculously difficult decision, I GOT THE JOB! He even let me know that he was leaning towards the other guy who had a lot more experience. Apparently, it came down to the video I made (which he had watched with his girlfriend which put her on my side), the fact that I had an internal champion, and the fact that I went above & beyond with the sales deck.

11. Focus on The 1%: Needless to say, I was pretty excited & looking back it wasn't one thing that I did but the accumulation of everything that turned the tide for me. Everything I did got me 1% closer to my goal and that's exactly how you should be looking at your sales process.

Little did I know that the work was just getting started but after a lot of late nights, it led to the best career year of my life & I was able to close 1M dollars in revenue in my first 9 months on the job. Well above expectations!

Also, to top it all off, one of the partners that I signed, Outreach.io, ended up acquiring our company less than a year later and now the sky is truly the limit!

I hope this inspires you to go out there, put everything on the line, and land your dream job!

Lessons Learned:

- Treat the hiring process as a sales process, because it is. You're selling yourself.

- It's not just one thing that makes the difference. It's the combination of doing all of the little things right. Be creative, pay attention to details and always do MORE.

- Passion (with a plan) trumps experience. If you can show that you're willing to roll up your sleeves, get to work, and approach the role with unequaled passion, you can beat out experience.

- Engage with everyone in your network as if you might work with (or for) them – one day, you just might!

IF YOU WANT TO BE SUCCESSFUL IN SALES, LIVE WITH YOUR IN-LAWS

By Evan Kelsay

Evan Kelsay was just promoted to Vice President of Enterprise Sales at Seismic after his record setting performance as a Senior Director of Global Accounts where he put up over 800% of his annual number. You can hear that story in episode 56 of the podcast (top1.fm/56). Evan is working on two other stories for Volume 2 of *Sales Success Stories*: The Era of Cognitive Obesity & another to be named.

Whttp do you need to crush your quota this year?" my wife asked me. "Time" I answered.

In 2018, I started a new sales job at a technology company selling enterprise software after over 6 years at my previous company and a decade in a different industry.

My wife was between jobs, we had toddler twin boys, and we were living short-term with my in-laws because we wanted to buy a house in the next year. Leaving the steady paycheck and consistent performance for another individual contributor role at a new company was a risk, but my wife knew a new challenge would be good for me and believed in my abilities.

I was determined to make this new move work, but I knew that running a great sales cycle (or a series of them) at my priority accounts would take time. Lots of it. Here's a sampling of what I believe is required during the Preparation phase before having even one conversation with the account ...

- Interview potential end users to understand their pain and what keeps them from doing their jobs.

- Perform deep research into the company's (and their competitors and customers) financials, presence on review sites, and job descriptions to digest and formulate a point-of-view about challenges and opportunities their industry and company faces, specifically what's limiting growth, ballooning cost, and increasing risk.

- Map the names, titles, and connections of everyone you think is on the buying committee (over 6 people and growing, per CEB), and everyone you think might influence each member of the buying committee, which is at least 2-3 people for every committee member.

- Interview channel partners of yours who do business with that account in order to understand how the account makes buying decisions around technology.

- Work with your marketing counterparts to run air cover campaigns targeting specific personas at that account.

- Engage your leadership, fellow employees, your network, and your investors to judge connection warmth of their network to the leadership at the account and where warm intros are most advantageous at each stage of the deal.

A mentor once characterized a great sales process as playing 3-dimensional chess, but you have to create an environment that allows you the time to play the game. Otherwise, the best you can offer an account is a compelling game of checkers.

After 2008 and the subsequent Great Recession, many executives wanted to reign in rogue spending and felt they needed more control over the procurement process for major and, increasingly, minor purchases at their companies. They put stricter formal and informal rules and guidelines in place for buying anything. Information flow to potential vendors was restricted; maximum-dollar signing capacity without oversight was lowered; and more formal, collective evaluation processes for purchasing were installed. The days of a single, autonomous decision-maker were long gone and in that person's place now stood large buying committees with an army of influencers. There are now exponentially more people you need to persuade to get a deal done in the modern era. (NOTE: Most of your champions and coaches within your accounts do not know this.)

Most companies have not adapted their sales model and resources to reflect this new paradigm, challenging salespeople to succeed at playing 3-dimensional chess without a rook, bishop, or knight. This forces most salespeople to be more transactional with accounts, because they don't have the time to properly prepare, focus, and execute great sales cycles consistently.

However, if you do it right, the account will perceive enough value in what you do to believe they are losing significant revenue and/or increasing cost and risk every month they don't have your solution. The cost of what you sell will be secondary to your solution's ROI. This is when it gets really fun. It will feel like you're speaking to your champions and their influencers as a partner who's on their side of the table instead of across from it. It will result in a deal that will transform your year and create a really close bond between you and your champions for years to come.

The downside is that you need a large amount of time if you are to do it right. I'm not such a Sales Jedi that I can crush quota AND be the world's best husband, dad, son, brother, mentor, friend, etc. For me, it meant I had to cut back on other things in my life to succeed at my job.

When I said to my wife that I needed more time this year to feel comfortable, I had the time I needed to crush quota, she said, "I'll handle everything else outside of work. Go get 'em."

And my family did – I didn't have to worry about paying bills, taking kids to the dentist, cooking dinner, selling my house, etc. I was incredibly fortunate that everyone was willing to pitch in, but it was necessary to succeed. I now understand why it's common in many cultures outside of the West for many generations to cohabitate. There's just so much that needs to get done.

Wait, what? Did you say "sell a house?" Yes, my family were such rock stars that they fixed up and sold a house I owned in my home state of Indiana without me so much as having to lift a finger.

In addition to simplifying my home life, I was fortunate that my new company's sales organization was led by grizzled, career salespeople whose philosophy was to give their sellers the resources below, across, and above them to in order delegate the division of labor necessary to surround influencers and buying committees.

With the gift of time both at home and at work, I locked myself in my in-law's attic (that doubled as an office) and got to work. Preparation. Focus. Execution. Remember that part in Forrest Gump when he finally breaks off the leg braces and sprints away? It felt like that. I ended up over 8x my annual quota.

Us sales folk are naturally social and easily distractible. Many of us don't have an army of family members to rely on or leadership that understands what we really need in order to succeed. My best advice is to simplify your life as much as you can to ensure success, because selling in the modern era is getting more complex, not less.

I'M A HUSTLER, BABY

By Nicole Miceli

Nicole Miceli is the top Solutions Sales Specialist at PULSE Technology, Formerly Des Plaines Office Equipment in Chicago. She was featured in episode 43 of the podcast (top1.fm/43) and is working on two other stories for Volume 2 of *Sales Success Stories*: A Social Butterfly's Guide to Successful Networking & Finding Your Tribe

For me, a sales career was never on my radar. I honestly had no idea what I wanted to do with my life, all I knew was that I needed to start *a career*. When the opportunity presented itself to me, it was a "here try this, and we'll see how it goes." I'm happy to say it's going really well, way better than I ever imagined. I also think that part of this is because of my 'hustler mentality.' What is the Hustler Mentality? I'm sure it has a different meaning depending on who you ask, but in this case, we will say it is a motivated person with the determination and persistence to succeed no matter what it takes.

It's because of my hustler mentality. I achieved one of my best deals early in my career. I was at a networking event one night where I met a woman, she didn't have a business card, and it was clear she was not there to mingle especially not with salespeople. A few weeks after the event, when I was going through my cards (yes, I know everything about that sentence is wrong, but we'll talk about it in another story), I decided to take a look at the card I was given from the woman standing next to her. As I was investigating the company's website, I discovered that the woman I had met was the owner!

The company checked out and seemed like it could be a good opportunity, so I gave her a call. In a very rare stroke of luck, she answered on my first attempt! Woah! I was super excited and then got shot down faster than it took me to dial the number. After that kind of call, I'm sure most people would have given up. I didn't, and here's where that 'hustler mentality' comes in, I called her right back. She answered again. I overcame the objections from the first call and tried a new approach with the second call. Guess what; I got shot down again AND AGAIN! It wasn't until that 4th call (all in the same hour) that she finally agreed to meet with me.

Now, to most people, calling and talking to the same business owner four times in an hour sounds completely crazy and frankly, it did to me too but that's what being a hustler is all about. I was determined to get an appointment with this woman because I just knew there was a potential sale there and I was willing to call her four times in an hour if that's what it would take to get that initial appointment. Thankfully I've gotten much better on the phones in my six years of doing this, so I haven't had to talk to someone as often as that to get an appointment, but that doesn't mean I've lost the hustler mentality. It's growing alongside me as my sales skills develop. Developing your inner hustler is an important skill to master. Do I think I've mastered it? No, there is always room to grow, but I do think mine is more developed than most because I've been working on it.

So how do you develop your hustler mentality?

First, you need to figure out what yours is. A good place to start would be to answer these questions:

- What drives you?

- What are your goals?

- Why did you set these specific goals?

- Are you willing to do whatever it takes to achieve these goals?

- What sales skills do you have that you need to work on?

- Who are your sales mentor(s)?

- Can you emulate what they are doing to succeed?

I could go on and on about things you should be focusing on, but you need to figure these out yourself and discover what makes you tick before you can truly hone in on your hustler mentality.

Secondly, having a manager that can help pull the hustler out of you and support you in all your 'crazy' ideas. I think that was one of the most helpful parts for me, was having a manger that supported me calling someone four times in an hour or supported me when a prospect would call in saying 'I was calling them too much' or supported me door knocking with little treat bags around holidays. She never told me that what I was doing was crazy, she supported my inner hustler and helped give me other creative ideas to get out there and get noticed. If you don't have a manager you feel can help with this look to your sales mentors. They are bound to have books, podcasts or weekly emails where you can get tips from, and a network of people who will be willing to help you when you feel like something you're doing is 'crazy.'

Third, surround yourself with other salespeople, which you deem as having a hustler mentality. Hopefully, you've already started getting yourself out there and networking, which would mean that you're meeting people in other sales positions. I think that these people can be extremely helpful, not only in helping grow your network but in showing you how they operate and what their inner hustler looks like. A rookie mistake that most people make is that they don't leverage the skills that these people hold. Look to see what their inner hustler looks like and what their sales skills strengths are and how you can implement that in your own sales process. This has been a super helpful tactic for me. One thing I've learned is that if you're meeting the right people, they are looking for the same things you are. Let them help you on your journey just like you will help them on theirs.

Once you develop your hustler mentality and finding that groove, you'll be pleasantly surprised at the sales situations you'll start getting involved in. Don't be afraid that what you're doing is 'crazy' or that your goals are 'too big.' Those things don't exist in the world of a hustler.

Lessons Learned:

1. How to develop and grow your own hustler mentality
2. Get a good manager or mentors
3. Surround yourself with likeminded 'crazy' thinkers
4. Find other hustlers who you can pick up good sales skills from

TEAM SELLING

By John Reidelbach

John Reidelbach is a top performing Senior Account Executive at Emerson. He was featured in episode 51 of the podcast (top1.fm/51) and is working on two other stories for Volume 2 of *Sales Success Stories*: Overcoming Obstacles & Always Answer the Phone.

As salespeople, most of us are autonomous by nature. We function best when left alone to handle our customer base. We know our territories best and have been working with many of our customers for a long time. If we need to bring in a resource, we know who to call. So why would we need to interject others into the sales process?

Take it from me; you can save a lot of time and increase your effectiveness if you form a team of sales peers and work together on strategic pursuits. You don't need to utilize this approach for all your pursuits, but I would venture to say you would be able to sell even more, and become more effective if you reached out to others in your corporation who could help you.

If you work for a large company like I do, you probably have different divisions, business units and maybe even different companies within your parent company. Keeping track of the sales folks in other business units can be daunting, especially with frequent transfers, retirements, hiring, and reorganizations. I am here to tell you that if you invest the time to build these internal sales teams, you'll reap the benefits for years to come.

In larger companies, there are typically other sales teams selling complementary products and services into your same accounts. These peer sales teams are a great thing because you can easily reach out to your peers within the other sales teams to share information. The three main benefits I have found by working in sales teams are sharing information about your common customers, sharing contact data with the members of your team, and collaborating on sales pursuits. I will share an example of how I used a team approach to advance my sales efforts.

Comparing Notes

If we're honest, we probably don't spend as much time as we would like in front of our customers. If only we could somehow extend the amount of time that we could be in front of customers or potential customers. By leveraging the people on your sales team, you can practically increase the time you have in front of clients. These individuals are probably calling on different individuals at your customer locations, maybe at different levels in the organization. They are getting different perspectives and are hearing information you may not know. Why not compare your account feedback to that of your peers to get a better understanding of your customer's comprehensive needs?

Contact Data

Have you ever reached out to a client only to discover they no longer work there? By sharing information with your sales team, you can better keep track of who has been promoted, who has been transferred, and who has left the company or retire. Having this second source of information has really helped me stay on top of my key accounts and how their organizations are changing.

Coordinated Sales Calls

Coordinated sales calls represent the most important benefit of working in a sales team. Once you've found a group of sales peers that share a common customer, work to align your products and message to add even greater value to the customer. This network of sales peers can really help position your offering as the best and most comprehensive solution for the customer.

I leveraged team selling on one particular pursuit in which the customer told me they had already made up their mind to go with the competition. Here, I had to think creatively and act fast before the competition received the actual order. I brought plant management into the discussion and showed how the benefit of using my product, and my company, was much more valuable than that of the competition. I showed this by bringing in the sales folks from other business units that sold related products and letting them demonstrate how our team offered a far more complete and valuable solution than the competition. This approach proved successful and convinced the customer to award us the order. I don't think we would have won the order had I not made a broader value proposition helped by my extended sales team.

Lessons Learned

- Invest your time in team selling. I say invest because you may not reap the benefits immediately. However, over time the relationships you have built within your team will pay dividends.

- As you start working with your sales team, you may feel like you are giving more than you are receiving. Stay the course, and you'll be able to gain additional information that will help you add value for your customers.

- If you don't work for a large company, network with others who may sell complementary and non-competing products, you may find you can share contact data and get to the decision maker faster than if you were going it alone.

TOP THREE LESSONS THAT LANDED MY FIRST BIG DEAL

By Jamal Reimer

Jamal Reimer is an incredibly high-performing Strategic Account Manager working for Oracle as an expat in Sweden where he is the master of Mega Deals and has closed three different SAAS deals each worth over $50,000,000. Jamal talks about how these deals were done in episode 61 of the podcast (top1.fm/61) and is working on two other stories for Volume 2 of *Sales Success Stories*: Even in Enterprise Sales, People Still Buy From People & Watch Your Flank.

Transitioning from selling for a small solution vendor to a huge global software brand can be a jolting experience. The first four years of my enterprise sales career was spent with three early stage software companies of no more than 150 employees. My experience was fairly typical. I was one of a handful of reps who banged it out of the phones every day, progressing conversations through the typical set of hoops: pitch, demo, follow up meetings, negotiate, and close. The deal size was $50,000 - $250,000. Nice enough.

I then started my first job with one of the largest enterprise software companies in the world - over 100 offices and 10,000 reps in the US alone, layers and layers of management, territory changes every year. It felt like moving from a small town to a big city. It was my first experience of a completely self-service culture. I remember sitting in a cubicle on a vast office floor, trying to navigate our internal online HR system to confirm my banking details for payroll. I wanted to ask someone for help, but it felt like studying in the library – a few people were around, but I didn't know any of them because they were in different business units. I just stumbled through the process and finally figured it out on my own.

The biggest change was the selling process. I remember going through my usual sales cycle routine for the first four months, and then I got an inbound lead that ultimately changed my life in terms of understanding how enterprise sales really work in the biggest companies. The inbound call was from a software company with 2,000 employees who were looking for a new CRM system. When we did some initial calculations, the value of the opportunity was 2-3 million dollars. That would be almost 10x the size of any deal I had done in my short four-year career.

Immediately there was a great deal of attention paid to this opportunity and pressure quickly stacked up on me as the rep from multiple directions. My manager, my VP of Sales and my presales director all started asking lots of questions and wanted constant updates.

The prospect issued an RFP with the goal of inviting a short list of vendors to on-site meetings to vet each product from top to bottom. The prospect said this would be the biggest internal investment in software, which this company had made in the past decade and would require approval from their Board of Directors.

Preparation

In a large software company even when a "small" 2-3 million dollar opportunity appears, the preparations for the RFP responses and onsite sessions are projects in themselves. CRM purchases are a big decision for any company because it is a core system that will be used by many stake-holders. Lots of features and functions for lots of stakeholders means lots of questions. The questions did come – the RFP was the size of a Russian novel. Fortunately, I had a very experienced team who had been in many similar opportunities and had seen most of the multitude of RFP questions before. We set about the RFP response with gusto. This experience was true war room stuff – eight people sitting in a room banging out question after question until every box had been checked, every question had a detailed explanation.

After the RFP was submitted, we soon learned we had made it to the short list of vendors and were invited to the onsite presentations with the prospect's CRM project team. In another round of preparation, the war room was again filled with product specialists coaching my presales resource who was going to be driving the actual demo. My manager was also coaching me to become the salesperson who would be delivering the intro and color commentary during the demo to point out value points and tell relevant stories.

The results of the preparation were amazing. During the onsite sessions, we were asked to demonstrate how our software would handle twenty use cases for stakeholders in sales, sales operations, sales management, and marketing. As we discussed each use case the project team would pelt us with questions, "what if we wanted to do an action like this," and, "can your software do that." This went on for four hours. We answered virtually every question with a credible response. I recognized many of the questions from the prep sessions – someone in the war room had seen that question before and made sure we not only had an answer but could contextualize the answer in the prospect's business. It became clear the project team had considerably warmed to us, At times throughout the session, I noticed two or three project team members, looking at each other with excited expressions as my presales resource described how our software would handle a specific situation. By the end of the meeting, it was clear there were simply no meaningful objections left. At worst they liked us, and at best they preferred us.

Visiting A Customer

One of the most powerful tactics that we used, and ultimately helped us to win the deal is that we had worked with one of our existing CRM customers to host our prospect for a half-day visit to discuss their experience with our CRM solution. This was an absolute game changer on several fronts. It got twenty people from the prospect to travel with us – a huge bonding experience – to the customer site by flying to another city, having multiple meals together and traveling by bus from the hotel to customer site and back. The moment we stepped out of the prospect's offices and began our journey everything changed. There is an immediate redefinition of a relationship when a physical journey is involved. You cease being "just a salesperson" and become a travel companion. In the airport, you might say "I'm going to get a water bottle for the flight, do you want one? Later the prospect just might reciprocate. Small interactions like this are powerful events that change, improve and deepen any relationship.

The visit itself was highly impactful. We arrived at the customer site and were greeted by our host, the head of Business Operations and owner of their CRM system. We were ushered into a large conference room and were served coffee and donuts (which I had pre-arranged and catered). The customer then led the session by having leaders in Business Operations, Sales and IT make 20-minute presentations about their use of and experience with our product. While the overall feedback from the customer was good, there were definitely areas of dissatisfaction or disappointment. I remember cringing and thinking comments like those would sink our chances of a win, but subsequent conversations with the prospect told a different story – the prospect's project team knew that no solution was perfect and the candid feedback from our customer, positive and negative, had given them a clear understanding of where the pitfalls and weakness lie. This was a key point for them because other vendors did not offer such a complete and candid view into their customer's experience, so they felt committing to working with any of the other vendors carried greater uncertainty and thus greater risk.

Informal Conversations

The customer visit yielded a third learning which was the *value of informal conversations.* As the trip helped deepen relationships with the project team members, it also provided settings which helped change the *nature* of the conversations we had with them. Sitting next to project team members on the plane or at dinner in a boisterous restaurant or at a late night out at a riverside tavern opened the door to a new level of frank conversation about the realities of the project, the players, their executives and the decision drivers more than any phone chat or conference room meeting could ever produce. Social environments engender interactions which are strongly influenced by on social norms which often include sharing little-known details or speaking plainly and without pretense or defenses.

Informal conversations during and after the customer visit revealed the concerns the project team had about our product and in several cases, they also suggested the support we could offer to help alleviate those concerns. Through these conversations, we were able to develop two "coaches" within the project team who we were working with to refine what would become our final offer.

In the end, we were awarded the prize and won the deal. The feedback from the prospect's GVP of Sales who was the executive sponsor for the project was that his team confirmed their strong impression that our software could do what they needed it to do (and much more). Further, some of the project team members added that after interacting with my team in several environments on and off-site, they came to understand that we were people they wanted to work with in the long term. He also said, "What really drove it home for us was visiting your other customer who is also a software provider like us. That gave us the comfort that what we saw in your demos actually works in production, which was the proof we were looking for before making a decision."

What I learned from this deal that has stayed with me ever since:

Preparation is the best way to avoid uncertainty both in terms of the depth of detail you are ready to discuss and your prospects impression that you have covered all important areas to their satisfaction. Uncertainty kills deals.

Visiting a customer with a prospect is a huge differentiator. Gives the prospect living proof your product works and gives you many opportunities to interact with your prospect off-site.

Informal conversations deepen relationships and are often the best forum for hearing the real story on the process, the players and details on how to win the deal.

If you would like to discuss and learn about sales techniques like those in this story, join us in our LinkedIn group, *The Sales Tribe*, the group for enterprise salespeople.

NEXT STEPS

This closing chapter is called "next steps" because just like in a solid sales process you want to maintain momentum and keep things moving forward.

If you enjoyed these stories and you want more, then you need to know that there are many more.

First, I would like to ask that you take a moment right now to write a quick review wherever you have bought this copy of the book. You may want to mention your favorite story and/or your biggest takeaway from the book in your review.

Next, you'll want to join the reader list at top1.fm/B2Bbook, and as soon as you do, you'll receive instructions on how to receive the video of your choice from the most recent Sales Success Summit.

From there I'd suggest that you subscribe to two podcasts. Sales Success Stories where you'll find deep dive interviews exclusively with top 1% performing sales professionals (top1.fm/subscribe), and Daily Sales Tips where we release a new tip every day, seven days a week in 5-10 minutes or less (DailySales.Tips)

If you really enjoyed these stories and haven't already read Volume 1 of Sales Success Stories - 60 Stories from 20 Top 1% Sales Professionals you can find links to all of the different formats and retailers at top1.fm/book1

Depending on when you're reading this you can either participate in the crowdfunding campaign for Volume 2 of Sales Success Stories in May 2019 where you'll find lots of preview options, great deals on multiple formats. Join the reader list for details.

If you're reading this after May 2019, then either look for a pre-order or actual purchase option. Again, your best bet is to join the reader list.

You're also welcome to email me, as I love hearing from readers and listeners. Please, don't be shy: scott@top1.fm

Finally, if you're serious about taking your sales game and results to the next level then why don't you consider joining us at the next Sales Success Summit? This annual event is rather intimate and features many of the top performers, including those whose stories you've just read. Top1Summit.com Beyond content that you won't find anywhere else from real top sellers, the goal is to deliver a memorable and inspiring experience. We want to help you find mentors and build relationships that will help you continue to grow in your own sales career.

Made in the USA
Lexington, KY
08 June 2019